JOURNEY INTO POLITICS

JOURNEY INTO POLITICS

Some Informal Observations

by

JOHN V. LINDSAY

DODD, MEAD & COMPANY
NEW YORK

Foreword

Most of this book was written before I decided to run for Mayor of New York City in the spring of 1965. The principal exception is the final chapter, which sets forth, in very general terms, my approach to the problems of American cities—particularly those afflicting New York.

I would have liked to devote some of this book to the tempestuous 1965 Mayoralty campaign and an even more turbulent initiation to the office of Mayor, but during the past two years there was no time. Writing is a uniquely difficult and lonely occupation, one which demands many more patient and quiet hours than I have been able to isolate.

I have, nevertheless, found a good number of rewards in writing, despite its exactions, for writing disciplines its practitioners; it forces them to clarify and focus their thinking. The process is especially useful to those of us who hold elective office.

v

Much of the substance of the book appeared in articles or book reviews I wrote, or in speeches I delivered, as a member of Congress. In the time I have been able to put aside over the past months, I have edited, rewritten, and extrapolated upon the texts somewhat freely.

The hours I devoted to the manuscript gave me a great deal of personal satisfaction, although so much has taken place since the original draft was written that the book now seems strangely quiet. Perhaps the strangeness is natural; compared with a single year's tenure as Mayor of New York, my seven years in Congress—with which this book primarily deals—seem peaceful, indeed.

In common with all first-time authors, I owe enormous thanks to many people for their encouragement and criticism, their help and advice, and their candid judgments upon the use of a semicolon or the strength of a thesis. Most prominent among them are my wife, Mary; my three brothers, George, David, and Rod; a former member of my Congressional office staff, Seth Tillman; my friend of a lifetime and the publisher of this book, Allen Klots of Dodd, Mead & Company; and my aide, both as Congressman and Mayor, James R. Carberry.

Some day, perhaps, I shall write an account of the 1965 campaign and my experiences as the chief executive of the Nation's largest and greatest city. If I do so, my motivation in discoursing upon the job of Mayor will be drawn from a quotation I only recently discovered, but will enjoy permanently:

"There is nothing so annoying as being obscurely hanged."

Contents

To M, with love

1

The Will to Run

I THINK I shall always remember my first run for public office more graphically than any other. I ran four times for Congress, and then for Mayor. Some campaigns were more complicated and more interesting to the public, but none stands out in my mind as clearly as my first effort to interest voters in my candidacy for office.

The campaign took place in the spring of 1958, when I sought the Republican nomination for Congress from the 17th District of New York City against the candidate of the regular G.O.P. organization. It was a bitter struggle and appeared at first to be hopeless.

I particularly recall a sweltering Memorial Day weekend when my wife, Mary, and I were collecting signatures from enrolled Republicans to place my name on the primary ballot. On a meltingly hot Saturday night, we had climbed endless stairs in Manhattan to push apartment house doorbells.

Doorbells are forbidding, impersonal things, aligned in conforming rows below identical Cyclops eyes in apartment doors. It is easy to forget there are individual human beings on the other side, each as different from the other as the doorbells are alike.

On this oppressively humid night of a long holiday weekend, the bells seemed especially forbidding and unresponsive. Few people were at home, the city was almost abandoned, and the prospects of my campaign looked bleak. I was totally unknown; I was running against the odds; people wondered why, and I had to explain repeatedly to the few who answered our ring.

Ultimately, we climbed the long back stairs of a building on lower Sixth Avenue. This time, the door was opened wide and we were given an enthusiastic welcome by a mother and her grown daughter. They were alert and intelligent, smiling and cheerful. The daughter quickly identified herself as a contemporary of my wife's at college, which became an additional note of unexpected good will. They had been following our campaign closely and were genuinely interested and excited by it—so much so that they volunteered immediately to work for my election. For the first time that night, we had discovered people who obviously cared about the election; more cheeringly, they sincerely hoped that I would win. Instantly, the discouragement of the lonely, steamy night vanished.

Although I have patrolled the corridors of hundreds of other buildings and pushed thousands of doorbells in five campaigns for office, I have always remembered their reception in those gloomy circumstances. Somehow it represented a discoverable concern on the part of people, repeated many thousands of times in different ways and in different places, that always made running worth while.

Why run for political office at all? I often have been asked that question, and the answer seems almost trite. It develops from a desire—common to me and to the majority of men I know in public life—to spend our time, energy, and such talents as we may have, in public, rather than in private pursuits. If the motivation is strong enough, we act upon it.

The war played a part in my entering politics, as it did with other veterans. A shipmate on my destroyer wrote me after my election to Congress that I had told him, one night while on patrol in the Pacific Ocean, that I intended to go into politics when the war ended. I have no recollection of the conversation, nor do I believe that such a course was clear in my mind. But in the vast reaches of the Pacific Ocean, amid long lonely hours on the watch, there was time for thought; especially as news came in of the deaths of classmates and friends. Consciously or unconsciously, there is no doubt that three years of active service in the Navy contributed to my decision. Postwar frustrations—the restless strivings to find direction and moorings—led me toward government service.

Then, too, there was the recollection of things said about public life and the public interest in school, particularly during after-hours bull sessions with contemporaries. Young ideas about public service tend to be smothered in adult life. I was fortunate enough to receive an excellent education and the purpose of this training came into our conversation more than once while my wife and I were debating whether I should run in 1958. Had I received the benefit of an excellent education only to pursue a private course? Or was there not some wider, more selfless objective, in the tradition of the English public schools? To a degree, this was the tradition of my preparatory school work at St. Paul's School in Concord, New Hampshire.

Finally, there was a terribly pressing urge to be where the action was. While the world and events moved all around us, I, and many of my friends, did not intend to be left behind.

A group of us descended on New York City after completing our graduate school studies. Several were young lawyers, combat veterans of World War II. Some, like myself, were native New Yorkers. We grew to be friends through law practice and related occupations and through our activity in the New York Young Republican Club, of which I became President in 1952.

We made speeches for various Republican candidates in 1947. I did a good deal of street corner and sound truck speaking, mindful of the discipline this form of oratory might give me for trial work with my law firm. Our candidates, since they ran in overwhelmingly Democratic districts, invariably lost. One of our group ran for Congress from Brooklyn in the Republican primaries during a special election in 1951. He was beaten. We supported others, and we campaigned for various reforms. We were an independent lot and we became involved all over the city. We were filled with energy and ambition and we had a thorough and deep-seated disgust with the way political affairs were conducted in New York City.

In 1951 our concern became national; we wrote a pamphlet entitled "Blueprint for a Better America," which purported to cover almost every subject of importance to the country, from foreign policy and the Marshall Plan to domestic health and education programs. At that time, it appeared far more ideal than practical.

We formed a group called "Youth for Eisenhower" and wrote letters across the country in the hope of interesting other young Republicans in supporting our favorite.

Mary and I traveled to Europe in the summer of 1951, carrying a letter from a mutual friend to General Eisenhower, then commander of the NATO forces in Europe. We drove out of Paris to Neuilly, headquarters of SHAPE—Supreme Headquarters Allied Powers in Europe—and there met the General. He entered, wearing his familiar Eisenhower jacket decorated by a single bar of ribbons. With his ruddy complexion and cordial smile, he looked very much the winner he was, and was to be again. We talked about NATO and his staff members from the Allied countries of Europe. It had been enormously impressive to see the British, French, and other officers of the Allied nations in the uniforms of their countries, under the command of this single American. Their enthusiasm for the new structure of NATO was contagious. It remained vivid to me ten years later, when as a congressional delegate to the NATO Parliamentarians Conference and as the chairman of its Political Committee, I joined the struggle against the threatened dismemberment of NATO.

Before leaving the General, I said that thousands of Republicans in New York and other states hoped he would be the Presidential nominee at the Republican Convention of 1952. He simply grinned, passing off my remark with a wave and negative shake of the head.

Many weeks later, I discovered that Herbert Brownell, an experienced, powerful leader of eastern Republicans, flew in secret to Paris to talk seriously with General Eisenhower about entering the New Hampshire Presidential primary. I did not know Herb Brownell until later, after the story of his trip was published.

With my brother David and several of our friends in the New York Young Republican Club, I went to the 1952 convention. We wangled our way into various volunteer jobs, and felt we were again a party of contemporary political history. Dave and I had been through this before; in 1940, when we twins were eighteen, we were page boys at the Republican Convention in Philadelphia. That was the year the galleries stampeded the delegates to Willkie, teaching everyone a lesson in convention psychology. I thought of it in San Francisco twenty-four years later, on the rostrum of the Cow Palace, awaiting my turn to speak while Governor Nelson Rockefeller faced up to the anti-Rockefeller animosity infusing the 1964 G.O.P. convention.

From 1952 to 1955 I was fully occupied with my law practice. I moved increasingly into trial work, which I had wanted, and my law firm had taken me into partnership.

Mary and I lived in Stuyvesant Town, a large housing development on the lower east side of Manhattan, where our first and second daughters were born.

In 1955 we moved to Washington, where I took up new duties in the United States Department of Justice as Executive Assistant to Attorney General Brownell. It was to be an exciting two years. I liked government and I was working for a man of enormous professional competence and political acumen. Brownell had assembled around him in the Department an able team, comprising men such as J. Lee Rankin of Nebraska, Simon E. Sobeloff of Maryland, Warren Olney of California, William P. Rogers of the District of Columbia (later to become Attorney General), Warren E. Burger of Minnesota, and General Joseph Swing, retired from a wide-varying army career. I found myself working on immigration and travel policy, on Presidential pardons, parole and prisons, on matters of concern to the Attorney General in the Cabinet, on legislation in the Congress. Three cases were assigned to me for argument in the Supreme Court.

Our third daughter, Anne, was born in our small house on Jennifer Street.

In 1957 I rejoined my law partners in New York City. I was digging back into casework when a party fight, smoldering for some years, flared to a head in Republican ranks in the 17th Congressional District of New York.

The District's general boundaries extended from the East River westward across Manhattan to the garment district and Central Park West, ending near Harlem on the north and in Greenwich Village on the south. The District very likely is the most dynamic, varied Congressional District in the country. It is misnamed the "Silk Stocking" because it consists in part of the high-rent areas along Fifth, Madison, and Park Avenues. But it also includes a part of Spanish Harlem and the Lower East Side adjacent to the Bowery.

The Seventeenth contains one of the greatest varieties of nationality groups of any Congressional district in the country. Its population is almost 385,000, and a surprisingly high percentage—more than half—voted in the 1964 general election. In party registrations, it is largely Democratic, yet it has a long tradition of independent voting. Its residents include leaders in every field—the arts, education, finance, communications, science, theater, business, and the professions. It has a larger international community than many capitals.

In 1958 the district had not been enlarged substantially by reapportionment. It had voted Republican by a narrow margin, but it was the last Republican-held Congressional District, out of six, in Manhattan, and it was endangered. One of the city's few remaining Republican state legislative seats had recently been lost. The country's largest city was nearing one-party status.

Seven of us formed a nucleus of insurgents, resolved to do something about it; we decided upon a hard, and probably costly, primary fight against the old-time G.O.P. organization. It looked difficult, if not impossible, to win. Even if we did win, we would go on to a larger fight against the better-known Democratic candidate.

Some personal considerations could not be ignored. It is

easier merely to contemplate taking an entirely different tack in life than it is actually to set a new course, particularly when you may make a fool out of yourself and probably your crew. I had just left a government job, and had barely settled back into a satisfying law practice. My wife had just gone through the process of moving our household back to New York, and we were meeting a normal share of problems in bringing up three small children in mid-Manhattan. My law firm partners were amenable to my running, but made plain their view that I might make a greater contribution to the community as an independent, professional man. Some held that politics, by comparison with law, was an accumulation of petty headaches—risky, lacking in substance, and intellectually compromising. I was acquainted with the low esteem that many business and professional people, often with good reason, assign to politicians. My own father, a broad-minded, sagacious man, confessed to this sentiment. As a successful businessman, who worked since the age of fifteen, he worried that I was making life unnecessarily complicated for myself, my family, and my law firm.

My father, however, lent cheerful support once the decision was made. He would stop every night at our campaign headquarters, settle in a corner and hand address a huge pile of envelopes. He always seemed to have registration lists from districts that were Democratic by about five to one, and my brothers and I remember him shaking his head and wondering out loud how it was possible for a Republican to be elected. Although I am sure he disapproved of some of my antics, as he did of some of my votes in the Congress, I had the feeling that my father was immensely pleased that I had accomplished what I set out to do, and that the registration lists did not prevent me from gaining re-election each time I ran. Nevertheless, he thought politics a transient vocation. He asked me once, shortly before he died in 1962, how many more times I intended to run for Congress. When I told him that I thought I was good for one or two more runs at the most, the nod of his head and the expression of his face indicated that he was reassured.

My father became lonelier each year after Mother's premature death in 1947. My campaigns kept him involved and interested, for they brought the family together in an unusual way. My father never lost his humor or his kindliness throughout all of the uproar. He was known affectionately by all in the campaign headquarters as "Grandpa," as he was called by all his daughters-in-law and his eighteen grandchildren. People of every age liked and respected him.

I am sure that my mother would have favored my running for political office, once convinced that I really wanted to do it. Like my father, she was cautious, but she had a roaming imagination and a lively appreciation of performance. Mother was a graduate of Wellesley, Class of 1911, and my father often teased her about it. He had not gone to college and obtained a high school degree only by passing a high school Regents' examination while he was working. Later he studied at night for a law degree, and obtained it, although he never took the bar examinations or practiced law. Mother was President of the Drama Club at Wellesley, and aspired to an acting career. She went to dramatic school in Manhattan after college and toured the country in stock. Instead of pursuing her career, however, she succeeded in rearing a family of five children in a crowded Manhattan apartment. Mother loved the theater, and was even more devoted to the New York Philharmonic and the opera, both of which she regularly attended.

My three brothers and my sister were enthusiastic about my running in 1958. They were careful and balanced in their advice, but left little doubt about their support. My brother Dave, who was in Washington as General Counsel to the Treasury Department during the Eisenhower administration, was frustrated both by the distance between us and the governmental limitations upon his participation in the campaign. He was for my announcing my candidacy.

Two very special people to me then, as now, were my senior law partners, Bethuel M. Webster and Frederic Sheffield. Like my father, they were skeptical, but like him they had the wisdom and loyalty to help me probe the rights and wrongs and ultimately let me make my own decision. Once my mind was made up, they actively supported my judgment. Beth Webster had been raised in the West. He early became a highly successful New York lawyer, deeply committed to his profession, to the New York Public Library, the Ford Foundation, the Association of the Bar, and other important New York institutions of which he is a part. A piece of his big heart, however, remained in Colorado, and his frontier-like individuality set him apart from more conventional New Yorkers. I recall his saying to me: "Each man must follow his own star." It was a comment that, coming from someone else, might have sounded commonplace; voiced by Beth, however, it carried a special and important meaning.

We went ahead. In January 1958, fully six months before the primaries, seven of us, including my brother George, began meeting in my apartment every week. Initially, the conferences took place at three o'clock Saturday or Sunday afternoon for about two hours. As time went on, we met more frequently. We became an informal executive committee. Each of us fulfilled fresh assignments between each meeting, and reported back at the next. The assignments varied from ordering stationery and arranging for telephones, to telephoning carefully selected names of people to feel out the possibility of support.

There were few pristine amateurs in the room. Each had been a part of the Republican organization at one time or another. Some still were. But in many respects we were completely different; our minds worked in surprisingly opposite ways. One or two were cautious—they saw pitfalls which, even if they were to be avoided, needed to be marked and studied. One urged damning the torpedoes with an immediate announcement. Another left us when it became apparent the majority wanted to go "all the way." He had too much time invested in the regular G.O.P., he thought, to waste it upon an insurgent movement. We often disagreed; sometimes the point of disagreement would recur at meeting after meeting. The meetings clicked along, nevertheless, even though my wife, if she should walk into the room, could instantly feel when we were stymied on a point.

Most of us would be sitting on our spines, feet sticking straight out in front, hands plunged in pockets—in utter silence.

It was hard to get people to line up in support of the campaign, both before and after I announced my candidacy. I suppose the experience is common to most party rebels. We found that the grip of the organization was not readily broken, except by a few close friends who had been with me some years ago in the New York Young Republican Club. Patronage, it has been said, is the adhesive that holds a party organization together. The adage is pertinent even if patronage is nonexistent, for there always is the hope of it. Even apart from this, the concept of political regularity becomes a way of life for those who have long labored in a party's local vineyards. "I'm regular" or "I'm organization" are the terms an insurgent is most likely to hear.

I was not, however, without sound, skillful, professional advice. Attorney General Herbert Brownell, my former chief in the Justice Department, was then and continues to be a devoted and wise counselor. I value his judgment beyond that of most men who have won similar stature in politics.

Charles M. Metzner, my predecessor in the Department of Justice and now a Federal Judge in New York, was my daily counselor in those days. He remains one of my closest friends. A third advisor was Joseph A. Macchia, an astute lawyer, who knew all the pools, eddies, and riptides of New York City politics. He was my first campaign manager. They were joined by a precocious, quick-minded twenty-five-year-old, Robert Price, who brought to us an invaluable genius for political organization, timing, and campaign strategy. His ability to follow through on details has rarely been matched in modern campaigns. Bob Price managed all of my campaigns for Congress—and my 1965 campaign for Mayor—after a heart attack restricted Joe Macchia's activity in 1959.

My brothers—my twin, Dave; my older brother, George; and my younger brother, Rod—enlisted early, and brought their wives. Among the staunchest campaigners, too, were my wife's parents, Randolph and Mary Harrison, as gentle and thoughtful a couple as their native state of Virginia ever produced.

Having made the decision to "go all the way," we swiftly organized ourselves for an exacting campaign. We took a small room in the Roosevelt Hotel in mid-Manhattan, called on the press, began recruiting workers, and appealed for contributions. From the registration books we culled the names of the enrolled Republicans in the District and mapped out our canvassing approach to them.

A primary is governed by the formula of "one plus one." It is won by personal canvassing—singular appeal for each single vote. A handful of votes may swing the election; hence every voter is approached as an individual, and shown individual concern. To win a primary in a political unit as compact as a big-city Congressional District a candidate should spend most of his time in personal, door-to-door campaigning. His workers, usually young men and women working in pairs, advance and follow-up his appearances. The most effective work that any person interested in a primary can do is to ring doorbells. Every voter soon can be identified with a category: "definitely yes," "maybe," "against," "tending against," "undecided," or "will be away." Absentee voting is not permitted in New York primaries. An August primary in New York City, such as this one, ordinarily favors the organization, because many people are out of town and the vote is light.

About a month after I had declared, the incumbent Congressman, Frederic R. Coudert, announced he would not stand for re-election. Two days later the leaders of all the assembly districts within the Congressional District met in the County Chairman's office. The meeting broke up without a decision on the organization's nominee. The delay gave us extra time in which to rally insurgent support. In retrospect, the delay may have swung the later election. We rang hundreds of doorbells during the week before the organization announced its candidate. He was Elliott H. Goodwin, an able and conscientious man who had given long and creditable service to the party, but who was the candidate of the leadership we were committed to upset. One heartening development at the meeting was that three District leaders decided to back my candidacy, using it as a means to strike at the County Chairman they considered ineffectual and unhelpful. The leaders represented only about one-tenth of the District, but we considered their endorsement a promising omen.

The most remarkable thing about the primary, as it gathered momentum, was the extraordinary response of people from every direction. It went far beyond our expectations. The array of talent that volunteered to work on various aspects of the campaign deeply impressed all of us. For example, a young man who walked into our headquarters proved to be an expert in telephone vote solicitations. In no time, he and three bright young women had set up an extremely industrious telephone campaign. The initial group trained a larger team in the subtle art of telephone salesmanship. Every evening, beginning at five o'clock, these energetic volunteers were bent over the phones. They were polite, and to the point. They answered voters' questions and when they did not know the answers they found them and called back. They kept at it each night for three or four hours. Their ears ached and their fingers were sore from dialing, but they enjoyed the experience, and they gradually gained good will and support for our cause.

Joe Macchia and Bob Price, who ran the headquarters staff, worked out the table of organization and assignments so that every one of the thousand or more volunteer workers knew at any given moment exactly what he was expected to do. They supervised the format and printing of all pieces of campaign literature and the coordination of mailings; the essential tasks of stuffing, addressing, and stamping envelopes.

Some time later I asked one of our best young workers what residual impression he took away from the primary. His answer was simple: "That it could be done." He went on: "The most extraordinary discovery I made was that people *do* care and that people in New York City in the middle of August *can* get steamed up over something other than the heat and the World Series."

Somehow, a chord was struck. It moved people from apathy to interest. Our canvassers very often recruited workers among voters whose doorbells they had rung. A lively girl who turned out to be one of our most effective campaigners was gathered into the fold in this accidental manner. She participated in every subsequent campaign. Friends from the suburbs spent days and nights in New York pounding the streets or using the phones. Their wives often pitched in. One commuter, a publisher, not only took on the responsibility for canvassing a sizable chunk of the district, but assisted me with speeches and statements for the press.

Most New Yorkers make the pleasant discovery, sooner or later, that New York is a montage of small towns, embodying the rural virtues of neighborliness—providing reasonable effort is made—with the urban respect for independence and privacy. Our volunteers learned that the majority of their neighbors were unexpectedly courteous and interesting. It was novel to visit their homes; it was absorbing to explore the neighborhood—often for the first time.

By primary day, August 12, most of us were close to exhaustion and anxious to receive a verdict. Macchia and Price pursued every last election detail. Price held a series of briefings with our volunteers, carefully instructing them in the business of poll watching. He explained the law, told them what their rights were, what to look out for and what to do if they thought they were not receiving fair treatment.

Nineteen fifty-eight was the last year of the paper ballot in primary elections—for good reasons. Paper ballots invite fraud—and primary elections, usually bitter intraparty fights where much is at stake, can bring out the worst in anybody.

We won the primary by a three to two margin. We were exuberant, but very tired from the strain of a four-month campaign carried on while we faced the daily obligation of earning a living.

We recessed for just ten days. By Labor Day we were back on the sidewalks gathering votes for a tough general election. The campaign went nonstop until election day, block by block, building by building. I held frequent debates with my opponent, Anthony B. Akers, and fielded questions from voters.

On election day we carried the District by 7889 votes out of 105,574 cast.

I ran for Congress three more times after 1958. Each was a vigorous fight; each of my opponents ran to win; each was a person of high caliber and competence, well financed and energetic. Each time, thanks to the skills of a progressively keener campaign team and the selfless energies of thousands of volunteers, and the understanding and favor of the voters, I substantially improved upon my previous majority.

During each of my campaigns, and in the equally busy intervals between campaigns, I would state my views on the issues. In the pages that follow, I have sorted out some of those ideas and thoughts for the record and for whatever interest they may be to those concerned with the art of politics and the science of government.

2

_____

The Congress,
a Middle Ground

I WANT to put in a good word for the House of Representatives. It was my home for seven years, and although I have squabbled in it, with it, and about it, I am deeply devoted to the House as an institution, one which has been described, somewhat loftily, as "The Forge of Democracy."

"No one pretends that democracy is perfect or all-wise," Winston Churchill once remarked. "Indeed it has been said that democracy is the worst form of government except all other forms that have been tried from time to time."

The average visitor to the galleries of the United States House of Representatives is appalled at its formal exercises in disorganized trivia, irrelevancies, "bunk" (the word was coined in the House), and at the aimless comings and goings. To the average political scientist, the imperfections of

the institution are manifest; they are democracy's imperfections.

Congress often is a prism reflecting the innumerable expectations, hostilities, and prejudices of the viewer. To Cabinet officers and Federal Commissioners the house on the hill
is a brooding omnipresence, hostile, immovable, incompre-
hensible—half asleep, yet ready to spring. The appointed
echelons of the executive branch, convinced of the righteous-
ness of their theories, spend ten months of the year looking
forward to the two when Congress is out of town. Yet neither branch can function without the other. Each learns to
measure the distance between them and to respect the other's
powers. The separation of these powers becomes very real
and very deep to those who try to bridge them.

To political scientists and columnists the House is a
crawling crustacean, encumbered by feuds, bad habits, and
narcotic legislative rituals. But to the late Sam Rayburn,
member of the House for half a century and Speaker for
two decades, the House was "the highest theater that any
one plays in upon this earth today."

Although I know that the root power in the House is in
the hands of a small group of party elders, I am generally
optimistic about the House's ability to adjust itself to the
times. Congress is more sensitive than many people and
most political scientists assume. With all its sluggishness and
faults, Congress, for almost two centuries, has made those
delicate adjustments that have enabled all Americans to live
together under a common, popularly sanctioned rule. It is
indeed remarkable that a country so young, diverse, and

energetic could have progressed so far with only one national conflict of such severity that it led to civil war.

The constant problem of representative government is to
find the middle ground between chaos at one extreme and
tyranny at the other. To the free man, extremes offer little
choice. The paralysis of uncontrollable factionalism is no
more palatable than the conformity imposed by an unrestrained majority. The role of the House has been that of
holding the middle ground—a role, by comparison, that the
French Chamber of Deputies over the years has not been
able to fill.

I do not mean to suggest that there are not weaknesses in
our Congressional system. Among them, I believe, are the
absence of continuing communication and information between the executive and legislative branches and the super-
ficiality of Congressional debate, especially in foreign policy.
As to the latter, the press often exacerbates the problem by
its often fragmentary or subjective recounting of Congressional debate.

Politics, aphoristically speaking, is the art of the possible.
So it is. But, as important as it is for reasonable men to make
reasonable compromises, it is much more important for them
to maintain a continuing reappraisal of established policies
and a continuing inquiry into their long term demands and
effects.

The functions of criticism and creativity in the national
arena are the proper responsibility of the party out of power.
A political opposition which fails of them, contenting itself
with negative carping, is failing its foremost obligation to

itself, to its supporters and to the American people. The function of the opposition is to oppose selectively, responsibly, and creatively. Each time a member of the minority party criticizes the policies of the current national administration, his criticism should express not only his view of what is being done badly or not at all, but also his view of how it can be done, or done better. A creative opposition, in short, appeals to the public mind and imagination by raising compelling policy alternatives.

The Republican Party has been the minority in the Congress for all but four of the twenty years since World War II. Few would agree that its record as the minority opposition was beyond improvement. Much of the fault must be assigned to the quality of the G.O.P. leadership in Congress, with its static attitudes and insular orientation. The party's lack of imaginative action in the House of Representatives, however, cannot be blamed entirely on its leadership. The Republican minority in the House has too often been handicapped by the refusal of the Democratic majority to allow it sufficient staff assistance, which is essential to the analysis of highly complex legislation. The Republicans, inversely, have not learned the art of using research talent productively. The procedures of acquiring information through committee hearings are haphazard, disorganized, and—in many instances—subject to the whims and eccentricities of a few members of special power.

A powerful and constructive competition for policy leadership between the majority and minority sides would frame issues and develop ideas far more vigorously than is presently the case. Presently, the debate on policy is insufficient. As a result of these and other shortcomings in the exploration of vital policy matters, the Congress has largely abdicated to the press a predominant role in appraising and shaping issues.

I do not believe that the kind of highly disciplined, ideological parties which exist in certain parliamentary systems could function in so heterogeneous a society as the United States or within our federalistic structure. Parliamentary bodies the world over, including their archetype, the British House of Commons, are reassessing their role and their "independence" from the government in power.

I think, nevertheless, that certain practices of parliamentary systems can be studied carefully, with a view to their possible adaptation to the American legislative system. For example, a great deal might be gained by the adoption—or at least the experimental adoption—by our Congress of the English practice of holding regular question and answer sessions in the House of Commons. During these interludes, members of the government, including the Prime Minister, submit to intense and systematic questioning by members of the opposition. The effect of the "question hour" is to compel both those in power and those out of power to think carefully and cogently about major issues of public policy. Questions—and criticisms in the form of questions—are put to the government primarily by the members of the "shadow cabinet"—the leaders of the opposition who would constitute the cabinet were their party in office.

In England, the question period depends on the existence

of the "shadow cabinet." It complements the actual responsibility of the government with the potential responsibility
of the opposition, showing the people approximately how
responsibility would be borne if the minority party were put
in power. The "shadow cabinet" system does not necessarily
guarantee responsible and creative opposition. It does provide a foundation for it, for which there is no counterpart in
the United States. While serving in Washington, I proposed
that the rules of Congress be changed to permit the Secretary of State to appear on the floors of the House and Senate
on a regular basis to answer questions. The resolution was
not acted upon, but I believe it would have done much to
achieve a healthy communication between the Congress as
a whole—as opposed to a few committees—and the State
Department.

In our system I would restrict the experiment, at the out-
set, to foreign policy and national defense—areas where the
Congress seems least informed and least equipped for careful, critical analysis. The faults are excusable; the complexities of both programs sometimes confuse their custodians.

A second innovation that would give Congress greater
responsiveness concerns the method of selecting committee
chairmen and ranking minority members. Under the present
system they are chosen by seniority. I see no reason why
they should not be picked within the committee itself, the
majority members caucusing to pick the chairman, the minority members meeting to select the ranking member.
Committee members know each other's strengths and weaknesses—both publicly and privately. They will choose well.

It is argued that this process will lead to more abuses than the present rule of automatic seniority; that highly imaginative members or members thought to be too independent will be bypassed in the interests of "the club," or that unscrupulously ambitious members might overly compromise themselves or trade away their votes on important matters in order to gain caucus votes. This is hardly a decisive argument. After all, the Speaker of the House, and the majority and minority leaders and the whips are elected in party caucus. Those selections have been, generally speaking, conscientious.

Books and endless articles have been written about the power structure of the Congress. Each seems to find something new inside its labyrinth, for there are a thousand combinations to the inner workings of the Congress.

The substructure of the House of Representatives is a subtle arrangement of clusters and "clubs." Its means of communication are informal, unwritten, and more sensitive than most people realize. Its functioning can be warmly personal and routinely coldblooded. Its performance depends in part on the personal respect members hold for each other regardless of party. At the same time there is rather constant friction between the back benchers and the front benchers; sniping between the outs and the ins of the ruling group on each side of the aisle. Often these divisions and pressures are more intense than those the public sees from the galleries during a major floor fight, with all of its attendant public drama. On the Democratic side there is the Democratic Study Group, a liberal confederation of younger Congressmen that struggles for recognition and voice within, or against, its comparatively old guard leadership. Generally speaking, the old guard is drawn from the New Deal and post Fair New Deal combination of big city regulars and southern traditionalists, with their common convenience of "safe" districts and consequent seniority.

On the Republican side there are several informal groups, or "clubs," each of about fifteen members. I was a member of two, the Acorns and the Wednesday Club. They meet once a week in a member's office, usually in the late afternoon. The members exchange information about committee work, trade ideas on means of communicating with constituents, and attempt to anticipate questions that lie ahead.

The Wednesday Club, the newest of the groups, received unsought but constructive press coverage when it was founded because most of the members were regarded as the liberal force on the Republican side. One of the original founding members was an unusually able and sensible freshman from Massachusetts, F. Bradford Morse, who had been "blackballed" from one of the other clubs for being one of the handful of Republicans who voted with President Kennedy to expand the Rules Committee from twelve to fifteen members at the opening of the 87th Congress. Almost all of us who had been temporarily placed in the isolation ward for voting "wrong" on the Rules Committee vote quickly became members of the Wednesday Club.

Communications being the essence of a Congressman's life, these "clubs," like the House gymnasium, perform a function. They provide the means of rational discussion among compatible equals. So do various other informal arrangements, at the leadership level or not, where a bottle is broken out and serious words are exchanged along with the banter. With rather few exceptions, Congressmen have a respect for each other, for each was elected; each knows, regardless of district, what one must go through to get elected. Hence there is between them an understanding and a respect, even when they have little else in common.

In the last analysis, virtually all members of Congress vote their districts. Stripped of all the explanations, all the maneuvering, and all the posturing, in the showdown members follow what they believe to be the general wish of their constituents. Most members acknowledge their essential provincialism; that is why they normally get along with each other; why the system works as well as it does.

Reapportionment, however, attacks the root of the system by threatening the security of members who have grown comfortable in their constituencies. It may change, sometimes basically, the district to which the Congressman owes his seat. Redistricting will control the future behavior of the representative and hence may dislocate his relaxed habits and his traditional stances. Some survive it. Some don't. Those who survive probably change their habits; the accommodation resembles a family, or a nation adjusting to a new generation, a changing technology, or the relentless transitions of time and history.

The House of Representatives is an institution slowly and constantly in change—although often undetectably to the

Nation—as people and time change. Service in the House is a continuing campaign: judging, testing, being judged and being tested. That is both its joy and its demand.

One has to enjoy campaigning really to enjoy the House. The members—all four hundred and thirty-five of them—run every two years, which means that they are running all the time. The average assistant secretary of this, that, or the other Federal department, in charge of moving national policy through the Congress, would be horrified if he could sit in on the average late afternoon bull session of an average group of Congressmen. He would find "the program" subjected to an average housewife's test that he might have overlooked in his industrious attentiveness to more high-flown theories or criteria. On the other hand it is his job to initiate, and let the Congressman enjoy the luxury—he may have few enough—of criticizing it.

A Congressman's life is in two worlds. Each is aware of the other, but hardly understands it. The world of Washington and the world of "the district" are wider apart, by far, than the mileage that separates them. It is the constant wonder of the shuttling Congressman, whether he comes from Peoria, Santa Fe, or New York, how divergent are the two spheres in which he moves.

Occasionally, however, the two worlds can be reconciled felicitously. Being an incurable theater buff, I once accepted a part-time role in an off-Broadway production of Stephen Vincent Benét's epic poem, *John Brown's Body*. My function was to deliver the opening, ten-minute narration whenever I happened to be in New York and could spare the time. Some months later, when I was running hard and on a handshaking tour in Greenwich Village, a woman, whom I met strolling with her husband in Washington Square Park, said to me, with a twinkle: "Mr. Lindsay, my husband and I saw you in *John Brown's Body*. We didn't know at the time that you were a Congressman, and we were so pleased to discover later that you had another occupation."

A woman once came into my Congressional office on West Forty-fourth Street in Manhattan during my regular Saturday morning "clinic" to complain to me that personal wires in her head were being tapped by the Central Intelligence Agency. She said she was receiving unauthorized messages. Congressmen receive many complaints of this nature. I have talked with many persons who were being chased, followed, invaded, or tapped. What was different in this case was her unique and wholly constructive solution. She requested me to ask the Federal Communications Commission to order the CIA off her frequency.

Another woman confided to me that she had received a message from heaven, informing her of her fated marriage to Joseph W. Martin, Jr., former Speaker of the House of Representatives, former chairman of the Republican National Committee, and a lifelong bachelor. My correspondent had been concerned about Joe's lack of marital status for some twenty-five years. She had never met Joe Martin, and Joe, upon reflection, had no recollection of meeting her. Joe was in his middle seventies when I put this proposal to him one day on the House floor. He pondered the matter gravely for a bit and then asked me to say to the lady how flattered he was and to tell her the following story:

When Joe was a newly elected Congressman from Massachusetts, and had served for a term or so, a group of his female supporters came to him one day as a delegation and counseled him that inasmuch as they wanted him one day to be Senator, Governor, or President, he really should have a wife. "People like their candidate to have a wife," they said. Joe consented, but on one condition. "I gave my ladies a list of the girls I was seeing and told them that if they could all agree on one, I would propose to her and if she'd have me, we'd get married.

"Do you know," continued Joe, "that fifty years have gone by, and they still haven't agreed on a name."

Despite its shortcomings and its massive frustrations, the Congress is an enjoyable institution. Being a member of Congress is, I believe, the most pleasant public office a man can hold. It's hard for a member who enjoys it to leave the House—and they all miss it, in a way.

Members customarily have two philosophies about service in the House. Some want to stay permanently, building up seniority as they go, content to adapt themselves after their first few years of freshness to a system that demands rounding of the edges and a careful adherence to the power structure. Others are not built for the leveling process that must take place in the middle years of a career in the House. I was in the latter category, which required that I return to private life after a number of terms, or seek another office. In a great many cases, no one can judge which course is preferable. I recall the advice a wise senior member gave to me the day I was sworn in and first met my colleagues in the House. He must have seen his thirtieth year as a member. "John," he said, "they'll try to talk you into leaving this place one day, into running for some other office. When they do, don't do it. You'll never find another home as happy as this one."

3

The Rights of Americans

THE FIRST order of business for any freshman Congressman is his committee assignment. He normally needs enterprise, finesse, and good breaks if he is to gain a committee of his choice. If there is a leadership fight shaping up as the House convenes, the new Congressman's initial decision on how he lines up may determine the course of his entire career. For his committee assignment is as important to the effectiveness of a Congressman as his campaign organization was to his election.

I aspired to Foreign Affairs or Judiciary, both major-rank committees. I knew I would be lucky to obtain either. The Judiciary Committee seemed the more logical choice, for the last election had brought about a vacancy from New York State, and my work and experience in the Justice Department made the assignment a natural continuum. It was rare that a freshman was selected for the Foreign Affairs

Committee. Besides, more senior members from New York State also sought assignment to Foreign Affairs.

The U. S. Attorney General, William Rogers, and his predecessor, Herbert Brownell, assisted my campaign for a Judiciary spot. Helpful, too, was the New York representative on the powerful Republican "Committee on Committees," Representative Catharine St. George of Tuxedo Park. Although we often disagreed philosophically, I found Mrs. St. George a charming and witty woman. When she rose to speak on the floor of the House, members listened, and with good reason, for she argued her points sharply and succinctly. The best debaters in the House thought twice about opposing her in a floor exchange. They ordinarily emerged as losers.

My assignment to the Judiciary Committee undoubtedly was a break of some importance. It was then that the nation's great legislative battles on civil rights were beginning, and I was in a position to play a possibly significant role.

At the turn of the decade, world-wide attention was rather suddenly focused on the swellings of the civil rights movement in the United States. The movement was to cause division and strife, but it was happening, whether it was liked or not. To avoid it was asking for eventual chaos. Both its merit and its excesses had to be faced. This may be true for some time to come.

Part of the merit was the need of a comprehensive framework of laws within which Americans, regardless of race, can enjoy their enfranchised share of the nation's promise of equal treatment.

It is surprising, in many ways, that these adjustments took so long. The Thirteenth, Fourteenth, and Fifteenth Amendments to the Constitution, amendments which were enacted by our country more than one hundred years ago, were made part of the Constitution specifically for the purpose of adjusting wrongs done to Negroes. And each of these amendments specifically provides that "Congress shall have power to enforce this article by appropriate legislation." The Constitution, however, is not self-implementing; legislation is required to enforce it. A series of largely ineffective and badly drafted criminal statutes were enacted soon after the Constitutional amendments were adopted eighty-five years ago. But it was not until the Civil Rights Acts of 1957 and 1960, passed during the Eisenhower Administration, that a really substantial beginning was made. They were followed by the Civil Rights Act of 1964, which took the largest step yet toward meeting the requirements of the Constitution. Its primary innovations were laws to prevent racial discrimination in employment and public accommodations.

Curiously, voting rights were neglected, and the omission had to be repaired in the Voting Rights Act of 1965. Another omission of 1964, which was not corrected in 1965, was the protection of First Amendment rights. That amendment unequivocally and absolutely established "the right of the people peaceably to assemble, and to petition the government for a redress of grievances." There has been opposition to orderly demonstrations, but that opposition cannot be based on a questioning of the right to demonstrate peaceably. There is no doubt as to the absolute nature of the protection given by the Constitution. Correspondingly, the public has a right to protection from violence stemming from demonstrations that become unpeaceful. These are delicate and important balances; they must be re-examined and reset periodically.

Local police powers to protect the public against violence or the possibility of violence must be weighed against First Amendment rights guaranteed by the Constitution. The right of peaceable assembly must be respected, no matter how controversial or unpopular the cause; at the same time, the public safety must be respected and protected. The rule of law must be adequate to do both. Arriving at a balance demands delicacy and precision, and both are elusive to the most conscientious practitioners of government.

It is strange that humans have taken so long to rebel against the suffering inflicted upon the possessors of a colored skin or an unfamiliar religion. Characteristically, and even uniquely, Americans respond to challenges of inequity and deprivation by assigning first priority to the relief of tangible needs. In a devastated and demoralized Europe after World War II, in an embattled Berlin, in a Communist-besieged South Viet Nam, our primary contribution to the struggle for freedom has not been slogans and promises, but the material wherewithal for self-help.

Certainly the realism and pragmatism for which Americans are known, and of which we are justly proud, is nowhere more urgently required than in the solution of the major domestic need of our times, the final realization for all our citizens of the benefits of the Constitution.

In making the adjustments required in our framework of law there was a good deal of concern that we were establishing precedents that would invade other fields. Many were concerned about invasion of private property rights. Congress, however, was acting upon decisions made by the country a hundred years ago in Constitutional amendments which put the burden directly on Congress to secure the civil rights of every person by "appropriate legislation."

One of the most controversial provisions in the Civil Rights Act of 1964 pertained to public accommodations— among them hotels, theaters, bowling alleys, and restaurants. Little was new about laws relating to public accommodations. Over thirty states had statutes on their books for many years barring discrimination in public places. These states based their statutes on the common law which our forebears brought to this country from England.

English common law on this subject is common law also in the United States and has a long history. In researching the matter when the 1964 Civil Rights Act was in early preparation, I came across a key English case decided over two and a half centuries ago. I took the floor of the House of Representatives one day to read to the members this language written in 1701 from *Lane v. Cotton:*

Whenever any subject takes upon himself a public trust for the benefit of the rest of his fellow subjects, he is eo ipso bound to serve the subject in all things that are within the reach and comprehension of such an office, under the pain of action against him. If on the road a shoe fell off my horse and I come to a Smith to have one put on, and the Smith refuse to do it, an action will lie against him because he has made profession of a trade which is for the publick good and has thereby exposed and vested an interest of himself in all of the King's subjects that will employ him in the which of his trade. If an Innkeeper refuse to entertain a guest, when his house is not full, an action will lie against him; and so against a carrier if his horses not be loaded, and he refuses to take a packet proper to be sent by a carrier.

I discovered also, and read to the members, this quote from St. Benedict on the same subject:

If any pilgrim monk come from distant parts, if with wish as a guest to dwell in the monastery, and will be content with the customs which he finds in the place, and does not perchance by his lavishness disturb the monastery; but is simply content with what he finds: he shall be received for as long a time as he desires. If indeed he finds fault with anything, or exposes it, reasonably and with the humility of charity, the Abbot shall discuss it prudently, less perchance God had sent him for this very thing. But if he be found gossipy and contumacious in the time of his sojourn as a guest, not only ought he not be joined to the body of the monastery, but also it shall be said to him honestly, that he must depart. If he does not go let two stout monks, in the name of God, explain the matter to him.

These points became relevant in the massive upheaval within the Republican Party on the question of civil rights legislation in the convention of 1964. An overwhelming majority of the Republicans in the Congress had voted for the Civil Rights Act of 1964, a greater percentage than on the Democratic side. But the debate was bitter, and it became even more explosive within the Republican Party after the vote was taken and the Act had been signed into law.

The Presidential convention gathering at the Cow Palace was faced with the question of drafting a platform plank relating to support for and implementation of the Act. The matter ultimately came to a bitterly divisive roll call vote on the floor of the convention. The Democratic convention later was to be faced with the same division, but it was less noticeable, possibly because the divisions there had a longer history. In any event, the debate in the Republican ranks represented a deep and turbulent division resulting from shifting currents throughout the entire country.

As an elected delegate to the Republican convention, I testified before the platform committee. If there was ever any doubt about the Republican heritage in the affirmation of civil rights, I argued, those doubts would be removed by a reading of the first Republican platform of 1851, especially this key plank:

"Resolved: that, with our Republican fathers, we hold it to be a self-evident truth, that all men are endowed with the inalienable right to life, liberty, and the pursuit of happiness and that the primary object and ulterior design of our Federal Government were to secure these rights to all persons under its exclusive jurisdiction."

The Republican platform of 1872 said:

"The recent amendments to the national Constitution should be cordially sustained because they are right, not merely tolerated because they are law, and should be carried out according to their spirit by appropriate legislation, the enforcement of which can safely be entrusted only to the party that secured those amendments."

And the Republican platform of 1876 contained this plank:

"The power to provide for the enforcement of the principles embodied in the recent Constitutional amendments is vested by those amendments in the Congress of the United States; and we declare it to be the solemn obligation of the legislative and executive departments of the government to put into immediate and vigorous exercise all their Constitutional powers for removing any just causes of discontent on the part of any class, and securing to every American citizen complete liberty and exact equality in the exercise of all civil, political, and public rights. To this end we imperatively demand a Congress and a chief executive whose courage and fidelity to these duties shall not falter until these results are placed beyond dispute or recall."

William Howard Taft campaigned successfully for the Presidency on the following plank from the Republican platform of 1908:

"We demand equal justice for all men, without regard to race or color; we declare once more, and without reservation, for the enforcement in letter and spirit of the Thirteenth, Fourteenth, and Fifteenth Amendments to the Constitution which were designed for the protection and advancement of the Negro, and we condemn all devices that have for their real aim his disfranchisement for reasons of color alone, as unfair, un-American, and repugnant to the supreme law of the land."

I stressed these precedents, as others did, at the 1964 convention, with no avail—and then recited the history of the

Civil Rights Act of 1964. This act was spurred to passage by liberal Republicans in the House and Senate. Its major parts were offered time and time again in the Congress long before a Democratic administration or a Democratic majority in the Congress had seen its way to move. It took Republican leadership in the Congress to bring the bill forth in the shape in which it was finally passed, all but bypassing the deadlocked Democratic power structure in the House. The bill passed the House with 78 percent of the Republicans voting yes. By contrast, only 59 percent of the Democrats voted yes. Eleven Democratic committee chairmen in the House of Representatives voted against it; the Democratic whip voted and spoke against it.

The recitation of this history before the Republican convention of 1964 was an exercise in frustration, already doomed to defeat. The convention, controlled by the New Right, was settling some old scores.

4

The Liberties of People

As a MEMBER of the Minority in Congress, with a large Majority whose whips took instruction from the Executive, I was especially conscious of the Minority's obligation to restrain the government from whittling down basic individual rights and liberties. The obligation applies no matter which party is in power; no party in power has been without excesses—excess use of government or Congressional power to impinge on individual liberties.

I believe that the real danger of increasing centralism does not lie in reasonable Federal expenditures for the destitute, for education, and for health, but rather in the pervasive threat to individual liberties that stems from any undue concentration of military, police, or economic power.

These liberties include the rights to speak freely, to dissent, to assemble and to petition and protest, to travel without harassment, to take up or defend unpopular causes, to receive the full benefits of due process, and to avoid the frustrations and arbitrariness of weighty bureaucracy.

Certainly one of the functions of the Minority in representative government must be to protect such liberties from erosion by the pressures of government.

Massive complexes of institutional power tend to roll up individuals in their path. This is true in both the private and the public arenas. The combination can be pernicious—as President Eisenhower warned in his reference to the colossal power of the military-industrial complex. Although most governments pay lip service to liberal dogma they seem unable to control the emergence of antiliberal forces in their midst. The more massive the government complex, the greater the possibility that these forces will emerge. They appear under various guises: "military secrecy," "national security," "international competition," "dominant governmental interest," or just plain expediency.

In 1962 the House Committee on Un-American Activities, backed by the Justice Department and the House leadership, tried to push through by unanimous consent a bill that went under the title of "Industrial Security." I helped to muster a small group which fought the bill in the House, winning when it failed to gain the two-thirds majority needed for final passage. The bill would have given the government summary power to remove from their jobs, without due process, up to five million Americans employed in private industry and universities on defense contracts or on related research. The rationale of the bill was that since classified information relating to defense contracts and research is spread all over the country in the giant industrial defense system and in universities, the government must have power to screen out from access to such information any person it believes to be a security risk. The decision not to grant a due-process hearing on some undisclosed charge could be made under the terms of the proposed legislation at various subordinate levels in the Pentagon. The bill made no provision for appeals to the courts in individual cases.

Three of us objected to passing the bill on the "consent calendar," a procedure that obviates debate and is reserved for uncontroversial "little" bills which are thought to have unanimous approval. It was then scheduled for floor action under "suspension of rules," a procedure which bypasses the Rules Committee and is reserved for relatively noncontroversial bills. Only forty minutes of debate is permitted and amendments may not be offered. However, passage requires the affirmative votes of two-thirds of the members present and voting. Six of us, all relatively new to the Congress, three Republicans and three Democrats, then went to work to muster support for an attack on the bill. We were required to overcome the Secretary of Defense, the Attorney General, the House leadership, and the entire membership of the Un-American Activities Committee under whose direction the bill was being routed through the House. We mustered enough "no" votes to prevent a two-thirds majority and the bill failed.

In 1963 the House of Representatives passed, by a vote of 340 to 40, an amendment to the Internal Security Act of

1950 which destroyed any semblance of due process for ac-
cused employees of the National Security Agency, an organization which handles highly secret military and Cold
War operations. The bill, which was backed by the government and the leadership on both sides of the aisle, denied
hearings and all other normal procedures which protect most
government employees discharged from the government. It
meant that any employee of this large agency who was
charged by an anonymous informer of having "wrong"
opinions, associating with "wrong" people, or any other
vaguely "wrong" activity could be summarily dismissed and
remain forever tainted in government files and records without any understanding whatever of why it happened and by
whom it was caused. It has been demonstrated repeatedly
that gross injustices occur when the government operates in
this fashion, and there is no commensurate improvement
in government security.

As disquieting as the bill itself was the procedure under
which its proponents originally attempted to put it through.
Despite cries of warning and protest from lawyers and civil
libertarians around the country, two attempts were made to
pass the bill on the "consent calendar"—which meant that
if no member objected, the bill was passed by the House—
without explanation of its contents, without debate on its
merits, and without a recorded vote. Admittedly, this particular bill presented a security question because of the
sensitive nature of the agency. But personal rights were
nonetheless diminished, and full debate was called for.

The Justice Department pressed continuously for legislation that would permit the FBI to tap wires without court order in cases "presenting a threat to the security of the United States"—a phrase so elastic it can be stretched to include almost anything. Improperly used, wiretapping is the worst kind of invasion of privacy. If used at all, it requires the most careful supervision by the courts. Modern electronic listening and eavesdropping devices have made the threat to individual rights posed by unchecked, unlimited use of this power all the more dangerous.

Some years ago my wife and I were shopping in Manhattan for a Christmas bicycle for our eldest child. We picked one out at a well-known discount house, asked that it be delivered, and wrote out a check. We were then led away to be photographed, presumably with the check across the chest in place of a number.

When we expressed our astonishment and offense, the salesgirl was surprised and said that all shoppers submitted to this when they paid by check; no one had ever questioned it before. It was, she said, a routine credit check. We tore up the payment and walked out.

In 1963 there came to light a widespread practice in the Pentagon of using lie detectors on Pentagon personnel. An entire unit did nothing but train people in administering lie-detector tests. In connection with a leak to a news reporter of a nonclassified Pentagon memorandum, the country was treated to the spectacle of a few layers of brass in the Pentagon, including the Deputy Secretary of Defense, voluntarily submitting to lie-detector tests at the request of an outraged and embarrassed Pentagon security chief.

Then it came to light that the National Institute of Health had one-way mirrors installed in the homes of newly married couples around Washington, with their consent, to study the effects on children of the "adjustment period" between their parents as newlyweds.

During an important criminal trial, the Justice Department was found keeping a twenty-four-hour surveillance on all defense witnesses, using short-wave radio and other devices. In another trial the prosecution maintained a post office "mail watch" on all correspondence being received by the defendant and by his lawyer.

About the same time, I and five other relatively junior Republican members of the House Judiciary Committee—joined later by a few junior Democrats—were barely able to hold the line against a bill which would have made it a crime to "obstruct" a government investigator in the course of his work. Under the draft originally submitted by the Department of Justice, an irate housewife who merely administered a tongue-lashing and brandished a broom because she objected to having her home invaded—or even an aggressive lawyer defending his client—could have been indicted.

At another time the House passed with only one opposing vote—mine—a so-called anti-obscenity bill, which would have given the Postmaster General license to prevent distribution of books and periodicals thought by any official in the Post Office to be obscene. The measure was pressed by a Republican Postmaster General and sponsored by a Democratic Congresswoman, accompanied by encomiums from

the Democratic Majority Leader. It was a major and probably unconstitutional assault by government on the personal
right of free speech.

The bill placed the full burden of proving innocence on
the mailer and attempted to exclude the courts from review-
ing the merits of cases on appeal. The works of Geoffrey
Chaucer would never have survived if such a government
tool had existed in the fourteenth century. The American
Book Publishers Council and other organizations finally
came to the rescue and the bill was jettisoned in the Senate.
A reasonable proposal was then drafted by a number of us
and enacted.

The House then passed, by a vote of 338 to 40, an ad-
ministration-sponsored bill which broadened the old World
War I Sedition Act. The Sedition Act, which had been almost dormant for forty years, made it a crime for any person in the jurisdiction of the United States to make false
statements designed to interfere with the Armed Forces, or
to attempt to interfere with enlistment.

The Amendment to the Act broadened the act to include
statements made by Americans overseas. The Justice Department thought it necessary because of our continuing
military commitments abroad.

Constitutional lawyers have claimed that the Sedition Act
is the most stringent curb on the personal right of free speech
ever enacted in our country's history, not excepting the
Smith Act. Under this Act, some may recall, in 1918 an
American woman was prosecuted, convicted, and sentenced
to ten years in prison for saying, "I am for the people and

the government is for the profiteers." Two years later, when passions had calmed, an appellate court reversed the verdict. A preacher, whose audience was a woman, two old men, and another clergyman, was convicted and sentenced to fifteen years for causing insubordination and obstructing recruiting by preaching and issuing leaflets on the Christian duty of pacifism. He was pardoned a year later. Under a state act, modeled on the Federal act, a woman was prosecuted for discouraging women from knitting socks for the soldiers overseas by saying, "No soldier ever sees these socks."

An area that was of special concern to me in the Congress was the use of confidential information in the administrative process. This is a procedure under which the government makes a decision affecting the life of an individual based on undisclosed information about the individual. Because it is undisclosed, he has no means to combat it. He is like the proverbial blind man searching for a black cat in a dark room. In discussing the problem in connection with proposed legislation to control the issuance of passports I summed up to Congress what I conceive to be the danger of such legislation:

The authority to use confidential information in the administrative process, under imprecise standards, coupled with the power to delegate the authority to subordinates, can result in a breeding ground of arbitrary action in the course of which innocent people may suffer.

Most people might agree with this statement as a matter of principle. Others might argue that the procedure is used in

other democratic countries in dealing with the question of
passports and other aspects of national security. This is relevant, but hardly material. Not long ago this country was
regarded as the cradle of a new liberty and we thought it
important to set up a structure which would safeguard our
liberties from arbitrary action by the sovereign. That structure imposed standards which I like to think are just a bit
higher, go a bit further, in protecting the individual from
the possibility of capricious or vindictive acts.

It is interesting to look back on the action taken by the
United States Commissioner of Immigration and Naturalization following the decision of the Supreme Court in *Jay v.
Boyd*. That was a case I argued for the government in 1956
while serving in the Justice Department. In a 5 to 4 decision
the Court sustained the use of confidential information in
connection with the Attorney General's discretionary power
to suspend deportation, under certain circumstances, of
aliens otherwise deportable. After the matter was ended the
Commissioner of Immigration, General Joseph Swing, a
man of instinctual rectitude, met the still-lingering problem
head on; he took steps to abolish, for all practical purposes,
the use of confidential information in this area. A later
check with the Commissioner's office revealed that no case
existed in which resort to the use of such information was
found necessary to a decision. This revelation demonstrated
to me that not only may the damage that can be done to
individual liberties under such procedures be all out of
proportion to the needs of the security that we seek to safeguard, but the corollary is also true, namely, that the ad-

vances we make in the safeguarding of individual liberties, however small, do much to strengthen the foundation of our liberties and, often to our surprise, do not result in any impairment whatever of our security.

There are other instances of whittling down individual rights and liberties. A recent development is the use of government leverage to induce people "voluntarily" to give up First and Fifth Amendment rights. Government employees, consultants, private citizens in contractual or subcontractual relationships with the government—a large and still-growing segment of the population—are asked to sign away Bill of Rights protections.

Regulatory agencies increasingly have moved in the direction of demanding voluntary waivers of rights. The Federal Trade Commission, for example, a few years ago mailed out mass requests to small apparel manufacturers demanding that they sign carte blanche "consent orders" binding them not to engage in the practice of sharing promotional advertising costs with retailers. Few if any of these manufacturers were under any charge of any specific wrongdoing. Admittedly, many manufacturers split the cost of advertising at the insistence of the large retailers, a practice which violates the Robinson-Patman Act. But the normal method of handling allegations of wrongdoing is on a case-to-case basis— complaint, answer, proof, and hearing. By signing this consent order, the language of which was unusually vague, the manufacturer voluntarily surrendered his rights to appeal to the courts from the terms of the order. Two thoughtful commissioners handed down blistering dissents, charging that this device set a new and frightening precedent.

Congress at times seems oblivious to the narrowing of our basic rights. Bills against individuals are routinely scheduled for consent-calendar passage until an objection knocks them off onto a calendar that requires fuller debate. Often they are brought up under rules that do not permit amendments. A favorite day for these legislative end runs is Monday, when many members are still away from the Capitol on weekend trips to their states and districts.

The structure of modern society, based as it is on a high degree of organization, encourages the growth of central power complexes. Today virtually nothing in the Constitution except the Bill of Rights effectively limits government power in any field. It is the final barrier. And even here, the wall has been breached, as the exigencies brought about by national security, international competition, automation, and population expansion have brought about pragmatic compromises of fundamental rights. Contrary to the common view, the Supreme Court has not made the protection of the Bill of Rights grow to the same extent as constitutional grants of power to governmental complexes in other areas. This argument was made by Yale Law Professor Charles Reich, former law clerk to Justice Hugo Black, in an article in the *Yale Law Journal:*

In a mass society, with access to information about what is happening in government increasingly difficult to obtain, with increasing monopolization of all the media of communication, and with heavy pressure for conformity from the large-scale organizations for which most people work, freedom of expression and political association are easily reduced to impotence. If it is true that they are indispensable to the functions of a free society, could it not be argued that the need for maintaining maximum legal protection of these rights has been greatly increased by modern developments? The Court has weighed eighteenth-century needs for rights against twentieth-century demands for power.

In those cases where the Court has "weighed the competing interests" and found the individual's interest greater than the government's, it seems strange that the Court should have been attacked for subverting the security of the nation. I should have thought the critics would take comfort in the fact that the eighteenth-century concept of individual liberty can be reconciled with the needs of the twentieth century.

William Pitt, standing alone on the floor of the English House of Commons in 1776, directly challenged the Crown's general warrants, which permitted the King's men peremptorily to enter a man's home. "The King may not enter!" asserted the great parliamentarian. Almost two hundred years later, the people who broke from the British Crown over the issue of searches and seizures have voluntarily submitted to all kinds of invasions of privacy which at other times in history would have caused the chambers of representative government to ring with protest. We find Americans in every walk of life, not involved in any crime or accusation of crime, submitting to or participating in fingerprinting, numbering, monitoring, "neighborhood checks," background and motivational research, or lie detector tests.

Our government was instituted to secure to individuals their inalienable rights to life, liberty, and the pursuit of happiness. In a society as complex and rapidly changing as ours, it is the highest function of government to safeguard those inalienable rights so that human beings may live in self-respect and without fear.

The Bill of Rights marks off a protected area in which each individual may develop and express himself in his own way. But even that area can be usurped in the absence of a vigilant and vocal public opinion. An absence of worry—and therefore of watchfulness—is an unhealthy condition. In a society increasingly given over to massive organization structures, in which individualism is regarded with suspicion or ignored as unimportant and unproductive, a sanguine confidence about personal rights and liberties can lead to the stagnation, and gradual vitiation, of the free system that our government was created to safeguard.

5

The Freedom to Travel

W<small>HEN I WAS</small> in the House of Representatives the government twice asked Congress for power to withhold passports from United States citizens. On both occasions, I testified before the Foreign Relations Committee of the Senate and the Foreign Affairs Committee of the House to ask for substantial modifications of the proposed legislation and, failing that, to state my opposition to it.

Does a citizen have a "right" to travel? If there is such a "right," what are its metes and bounds? These questions were cast into special prominence by the Kent, Briehl, and Dayton Cases, decided by the Supreme Court in June 1958, and later by the Zemel Case in 1965. The Court did not decide the first three cases on constitutional grounds. It held only that Congress had not given the Secretary of State "authority" to withhold passports from citizens "because of their beliefs or associations."

The State Department has been trying sporadically ever since to gain authority to deny passports in this arbitrary fashion. One day, perhaps, the Supreme Court will declare that the right to travel is surrounded with the First Amendment protection of free speech. How can people communicate if they cannot travel, whether across a street or an ocean?

The State Department has made exceptions from its general rules in certain individual cases. Once, after I threatened a vigorous protest on the floor of the House, the Department reversed its earlier refusal to validate a passport to Albania for a constituent of mine. He is an author who had contracted to travel by ship through the Greek Isles in the company of British scholars and students of Greek civilization. The port of Durrës, Albania, was to be a one-day stop to see some of the finest Grecian period ruins of all. The predicament of the single American on board would have presented a fine picture of American foreign policy as he stood on the gangplank—his passport surrendered to the captain on United States Government instructions—while his British counterparts departed for the short bus trip, passports and notebooks in hand.

The theory of the Department's position was that, since the United States does not have relations with Albania, it will not allow a citizen to travel in Albania, for his own protection. But the Department will make exceptions to its blanket area travel ban whenever, in its sole judgment, it finds the cause worthy. According to State Department practice, a citizen's interest in the distribution of an estate in

Albania would come under the exception—which means that a legacy of rare books on Greek mythology would qualify, but a scholar's interest in seeking the original works would not.

When one is talking about the sovereign and its powers, the word "authority" means different things under different circumstances. What does it mean in this instance?

The Supreme Court has said: "We deal here with a constitutional right of the citizen, a right which we assume the Congress will be faithful to respect. . . . The right to travel is part of the 'liberty' of which a citizen cannot be deprived without the due process of law of the Fifth Amendment." The dictum may give us the dimensions of the playing field, but it does not tell us much about the ground rules of the game.

The difficulty I had with the requests of the government for passport legislation in 1959 and 1960 originated with two proposals. One would have granted the Secretary of State the power to withhold passports from citizens where it was "determined upon substantial grounds that their activities or presence abroad or their possession of a passport would . . . (a) seriously impair the conduct of the foreign relations of the United States, or (b) be inimical to the security of the United States." The second proposal would have permitted the Passport Hearing Board of the Department of State, in determining an application for a passport, to consider nonrecord (undisclosed) information. The Board would be required to furnish a résumé of the confidential information to the applicant and certify it as a fair résumé.

The findings, conclusions, and recommendations of the Board would be transmitted to the Secretary of State, who would make a final determination. The Secretary, if he should deem it vital to the national security or the conduct of foreign affairs, also would have been empowered to consider nonrecord information, whether contained in the résumé or not. Presumably, under the general rules and regulations of the Department of State, the Secretary would not have been obliged personally to consider the case but could have delegated the authority, including that of resorting to confidential information, to a subordinate officer. There was provision for appeal to the United States District Court for the District of Columbia, but the Court would not have been given access to undisclosed information and would have been required to accept the résumé provided by the Board. There was no definition of the circumstances under which confidential information could have been used, such as on certification by a senior officer of the State Department that its disclosure would expose so-called "double" or "buried" agents of tested and known reliability, that the case could not be decided without the use of such information, and that the decision as to the need for both its use and its secrecy had been made by a top officer of the Department of State. The power thus reserved to the Department was sweeping and final, its exercise not subject to scrutiny either by the applicant for a passport or a judicial tribunal.

On behalf of the legislation, a State Department spokesman cited examples where the Department had been required, as a result of the Supreme Court decisions, to issue

passports to known members of the Communist Party. One
or two were admitted members with long histories of at-
tendance at various international Communist meetings and
functions. The State Department argued that personal communication by travel is the most effective way for any person or group to do business, whether it be the United States
Government, United States Steel Company, two individuals
trying to make a contract for the sale of paper clips, or members of the international Communist movement. What was
needed, therefore, it was argued, was authority in the State
Department first, to refuse to issue passports on the broad
ground that their issuance would impair the conduct of foreign relations or be inimical to national security, and, second, to act as sole judge, in many cases, of what impairs or
what is inimical, because neither the applicant nor a court
would be allowed access to the evidence. The rationale for
this approach was stated by the Department as follows: "By
so doing we can very seriously hinder the effective operation
of the Communist Party both here and abroad by making it
difficult for the supporters of that party to depart from the
United States."

Justice Felix Frankfurter was fond of the aphorism, "Let's
not throw out the baby with the bath water." Important as
the need for vigilance is, we should not be so overcome by
fear and mistrust that we lose precious ground gained in the
ancient struggle for freedom. The Congressional role, faced
with an executive demand for power, is to etch out legislative standards which, while giving due regard to the national danger presented, at the same time preserve and

safeguard to each individual his liberties. In certain cases there have to be restrictions on personal freedoms, in the interests of society, but they should in each case be carved out with a fine scalpel, not a machete. The classic example is that of the man who falsely shouts "Fire!" in a crowded theater. He can be arrested for doing so, and should be, because in this instance the protection of the group's safety supersedes the protection of the man's right—even though under other circumstances he would be permitted to speak falsely.

Similarly, there can be, under certain, extreme circumstances, a limitation on the right to travel freely. But those circumstances are difficult to define.

What is the right to travel? In my scale of values, it is one of our most fundamental liberties. The Supreme Court tells us that it is "part of the 'liberty' protected by the due process clause of the Fifth Amendment." The Solicitor General of the United States conceded as much in his argument before the Court in the Kent and Dayton Cases. But I would suggest also that it is inseparable from the First Amendment's sanction of freedom of speech and assembly.

Of all the freedoms we possess, the one we should defend above all others is freedom of speech. Speech is communication, and if the means of communication are denied there is a denial of speech. The Supreme Court has recognized throughout its history that denial of the appropriate means of communication may abridge free speech.

The abridgement of free speech is precisely what was sought by the proposed passport legislation. So, I argued, let's recognize it for what it is, and then see how far we must go to find a reasonable balance between the competing interests of national security and the individual's right to communicate by travel.

It should be clear that this discussion did not involve anyone under indictment for the commission of any crime, or under restraining order of any kind by any court, or stripped of any right or liberty by due process of law. The power to withhold passports in these cases is clear. What, then, of the admitted or identifiable Communist?

There may be risks inherent in allowing a member of the Communist Party, or one identified as such by our intelligence units, to travel abroad. But it should be pointed out that Communists travel from Chicago to New York or from New York to the Bahamas, or from Dallas to Mexico, or from San Francisco to Buenos Aires or to any South American country. None of these trips requires a passport for exit or entry, and the State Department quite logically supports this policy. It would be highly illogical for the department to take the position that Communists are free to travel to Argentina, but not Portugal.

The elimination of passports between this country and Canada, and Central and South America, and all the contiguous islands was consistent with the general benefit to be gained by eliminating unnecessary barriers to travel. In the 85th Congress, for example, following an administration request in support of greater ease and freedom of travel, the requirement of fingerprinting was eliminated from the McCarran-Walter Immigration Act for all transients and temporary visitors. With modern advances in travel and communication, and the expectation of greater miracles to come, the world has shrunk and distances mean nothing. It means little more to fly from New York to Paris or Vienna than it does to fly to San Francisco. Therefore, until passports are abolished under reciprocal arrangements with all countries—a development which one day could come about —passports remain important.

What, then, is the nature of the passport? Passports have been employed by our government only since World War I. Prior to that time we got along without them mainly because they were not a requirement of travel abroad. After World War I the citizen's request for a passport was generally regarded as nothing more than a request for a service from his government to facilitate his travel in other lands—something which governments have an obligation to do for all citizens.

The right to a passport has always been assumed to be subject to the general war power. Few would argue that in the case of armed hostilities there are not extraordinary powers lodged in the sovereign to place limitations on all of our constitutional liberties, limitations which in the absence of the war power would be unconstitutional. The history of limitations over the right of exit goes back in the common law to the writ *ne exeat regno* under which the English Kings could prohibit a man's departure or recall him if he had gone abroad. It was identified with war and service in the King's armies.

In more modern times, it became a formal credential to expedite travel. But after 1941, the crucial function of the passport in this country became a control over exit; the earlier purpose of the passport—to facilitate travel—became subordinate to the purpose of restricting travel.

What, then, of the First Amendment? Although constitutional sources do not reveal that the First Amendment was framed specifically to preserve a right to travel, they do not reveal the contrary. They strongly suggest, at least, that early Americans recognized a freedom to move beyond national frontiers. However uncertain its basis may have been, however unclear its limitations, the English recognized that freedom long before they crossed the Atlantic.

The people of the colonies, moreover, evidently took the freedom for granted: Witness the constant movement between colonies and to the West. That may explain why the freedom was not more clearly recognized in writing. The Declaration of Independence goes no further than to list as a grievance the restrictions which George III placed upon emigration. The Articles of Confederation merely guaranteed free movement between different colonies, though the colonies, not yet joined in a "more perfect Union," were more like foreign countries to each other than the United States are today. Perhaps the most direct documentary evidence is to be found in the Pennsylvania Constitution of 1790 which declared "that emigration from the State shall not be prohibited."

These sources, taken together, and viewed in the light of the Ninth Amendment, warrant the assumption that omission of the words "right to travel" was not intended to eliminate the right. Nor is the omission inconsistent with a specific intention to include the right in free speech. The Constitution was designed to guide the United States for an indefinite period of time. It would have been impossible to enumerate the variety of ways in which free speech might be abridged—and the framers recognized this in the scope of the First Amendment's language.

The liberty guaranteed by the Constitution is not absolute—"Civil liberties," says the Supreme Court, "imply the existence of an organized society maintaining public order without which liberty itself would be lost in the excesses of unrestrained abuses." Freedom to travel, like other liberties, is subject to reasonable regulation and control in the interests of foreign policy and the public welfare. The Supreme Court in 1965 in the Zemel Case upheld the State Department's exercise of power in refusing to validate passports of U.S. citizens for travel to Cuba. I am not sure that it is possible to draw up absolutely fixed rules which will in advance strike a proper balance which will meet the exigencies of every case, protect the public interest, and yet stay within constitutional limitations. Circumstances and the times vary and "due process of the law has never been a term of fixed and variable content." But the following general rules I would deem to be guideposts which should guide the Congress in the likely event that the subject is raised there again:

First, the right to travel—to communicate—is a constitutionally protected right which may not be abrogated by the State except under the general war power, which normally may be invoked only in time of extreme emergency. The right is a concomitant of the First Amendment to the Constitution. A denial of a passport, therefore, may result in violations of both the Fifth and First Amendments.

Second, neither the right of the citizen to have issued, nor the right of the Secretary of State to deny issuance of, a passport is an absolute right.

Third, the general standard whereby the Secretary of State may deny the issuance of a passport whenever he finds it inimical to the national security of the United States is too indefinite. In the past we have too often seen examples of executive arbitrariness under the umbrella of "the national security." Area travel bans placed on the whole citizenry may be reasonable under circumstances amounting to exercise of the general war power. Its over-use can be self-defeating.

Fourth, a refusal to issue a passport may not rest upon confidential, undisclosed information, employed under an unlimited authority, as such a refusal would, in all probability, be a denial of due process of law under the Fifth Amendment. I have spoken here of blanket, unlimited authority. There may be room for an exception to cover the hard-core Communist case, under which the Secretary of State or the Under Secretary, personally, will certify that disclosure will expose a "double" or "buried" agent of tested and known reliability, that such exposure will be prejudicial to the national interest, and that the case may not be decided without resort to such evidence. But even then, full access to the evidence in question should be given to the Court, under seal, for examination by the Court en camera.

The Universal Declaration of Human Rights is a document of great importance, seldom invoked. Article 13 of the Declaration states:

(1) Everyone has the right to freedom of movement and residence within the borders of each state. (2) Everyone has the right to leave any country, including his own, and to return to his country.

The United States has pledged itself to achieve, in cooperation with the United Nations, the promotion of universal respect and observance of the human rights and fundamental freedoms set forth in the Declaration. The United States should be faithful to that pledge.

6

The Supreme Court, an Element of Equilibrium

During my first two terms in Congress, the Supreme Court was in constant controversy. Almost weekly, some member of the Senate or House would take the floor to denounce one of the Court's decisions. In my last two terms the antagonism abated, but still smoldered.

Undoubtedly, the splits within the Court contributed to the controversy. It was clear that the bitter disputes that surfaced in public view did not help the Court in the Congress.

I'm vulnerable to the criticism that my concern for the Court as an institution has made me too much its defender. I have defended the Court even when it was quite fairly subject to criticism. I defended its early decisions barring prescribed prayers from public schools, when I felt that, sound as the general principle of separation of Church and State may be, the Court could have selected a better case on which to base its policy, and could have in the process more clearly formed a reasonable middle position. Actually the middle position was there, but one has to search for it, extract it from all the rhetoric. This we did when we fought in the House Judiciary Committee against amendments that would have written into the Constitution a specific provision permitting prescribed prayers in tax-supported schools.

I'm not a keeper of letters, nor a collector of memorabilia, but I have retained, and I treasure, the handwritten notes from Justice Felix Frankfurter complimenting me on my arguments to the Court in two of the three cases that I argued for the government. There is a tradition and a majesty about the Supreme Court, and its building, that is deeply impressive and unforgettable. Most people are propelled to their feet by their own reflex, barely touched off by the rap of the gavel and the clerk's cry, when the Court enters. The lawyer arguing before the Court must know his case, and the history of every case having a bearing on his. Government lawyers, especially, are expected to carry their arguments with insight and brevity. Even the most responsible critic is bound to sense the sweep of the Court's knowledge and thought after hearing its probe into argument of counsel for both sides.

Although its integrity is revered by those who come before it, since World War II the Court has been the target of intense criticism from beyond the bench. When an entirely reasonable pay increase for the members of the Court was before the House in 1965, it was defeated in a roll call vote. There was a mixture of motivations in members' votes, as usual, but probably the Court's entry into the sensitive area of reapportionment had as much to do with the defeat as anything.

The problem, it seems to me, lies with the legislatures more than with the Court. Whenever in our history state legislatures and the national legislature for one reason or another have equivocated and refused for long periods of time to make adjustments for the protection of minorities, or of majorities for that matter, the Court has found it necessary to fill the vacuum. It has been ever thus in our history. The Court has taken up the slack when the legislatures drooped, or provided the elastic when tensions between warring groups were coming close to the breaking point. It might not have been necessary for the Court to strike down racial segregation in schools if Congress and state legislatures had been willing to act. If state legislatures had been willing to adjust their systems of representation to keep them reasonably reflective of the urban explosion, the Court might well have found it unnecessary and undesirable to enter the field as a simple matter of policy. The question is: How long can the public business be left unattended in a democracy before something breaks? The Court in history has been required to put oil in the machinery of government when the gears failed to mesh and they started to grind. Each time, however, it has set off an uproar.

Then there has been the troublesome problem of finding the balance between the needs of national security and individual rights and liberties. Here the Court has been required to decide the question, because the issue was the power of the state—versus the individual. But again, largely because it has resolved the question in favor of the individual rather than the state, and questions of security were involved, it touched off a long and acrimonious debate.

I suspect it is risky to rely too completely on the cyclical nature of controversy over the Supreme Court. I am persuaded that free institutions and basic liberties do not maintain themselves and that the struggle for their independence and safety is unending. The mere fact that the Bill of Rights is permanently enshrined in the Archives Building ensures us absolutely nothing. I fear that our basic rights are more in danger of being whittled away bit by bit almost without our knowing it than they are of being destroyed by any dramatic assault upon them.

The Supreme Court does not go about blithely creating constitutional dilemmas for itself. The Court did not give the Negro darker skin than the Caucasian. It did not plant in the minds of Communist leaders a thirst for world domination. In answer to those who are passionately opposed to the Court, it seems only to feed the flames of impassioned statement to comment that the Court *must* cut new paths in resolving the deep social and political clashes that are put before it. These are clashes which are themselves made inevitable by the inexorable passage of time and the movement of history. And just as inevitably those paths lead across political soil. But if this be trespass, then time has stopped and the human situation remains frozen and unchanged.

In past years and even today the search for individual and collective security reaches such proportions that the preservation of the status quo has become a national craving. Material well-being, the sheltered life, and conformity blank out everything else. We assume that we will live forever and that what was good for us is necessarily good for our children and our grandchildren.

I do not mean to say here that in seeking new adjustments, in keeping with a changing world, the Courts, or the Supreme Court, are infallible. Far from it. Their decisions are often quite properly subject to strong criticism, but there is need for restraint. I used to say that as a legislator I reserved the right to be foolish. And as a human being, I also reserved the right to be nettled when the Court pointed out the error of my ways. But I could express my disagreement publicly—a prerogative that is not directly available to the Courts. This is a distinction which legislators will do well to remember, along with the realization that the function of a judge is quite different from that of a legislator or administrator.

To the legislator, I suppose that Justice Holmes ought to be the ideal justice. Alpheus Mason puts it this way, bringing in a rather well-known remark of Holmes's: ". . . Having himself no infallible measure of right or wrong, he (Holmes) upheld the programs and policies of legislators even though he considered them in error or foolish. As he himself said, 'I am so skeptical as to our knowledge about the goodness and badness of laws that I have no practical criterion except what the crowd wants. Personally I bet that the crowd if it knew more wouldn't want what it does—but that is immaterial.'

"Holmes was asked by a friend one day if he had ever worked out any general philosophy to guide him in the exercise of the judicial function. 'Yes,' the aged jurist replied. 'Long ago I decided that I was not God. When a state came in here and wanted to build a slaughter house, I looked at the Constitution and if I couldn't find anything in there that said a state couldn't build a slaughter house I said to myself, if they want to build a slaughter house, dammit, let them build it.' "

This would indicate a degree of judicial restraint that legislators would find admirable. It is, I submit, a restraint that tempers the Court far more than is generally recognized. And Holmes, like the present Court, was progressive in his interpretation of the Constitution and laws when the individual and personal liberties of human beings were at stake.

The briefest examination of previous uproars over the Supreme Court supports the axiom that "time has upset many fighting faiths"; that much more is at stake in the present-day consternation about the Court than the reconsideration of a few decisions.

It is worth remembering, for example, that the political hostility surrounding the Supreme Court at the time of *Marbury v. Madison,* which established the right of judicial review of an Act of Congress, was such that the new President, Jefferson, had refused to permit the Secretary of State to appear in the proceedings. The new Congress had not only repealed the Judiciary Act of 1801, defying Marshall and the Court, but even went so far as to legislate out of existence all terms for the Supreme Court scheduled for 1802. After this, when Marshall still had the audacity to hand down his opinion, now universally hailed, public statements condemning the Court crowded in from every direction. The following excerpt from a contemporary letter to an editor is a mild example:

Is it right, sir, that an extra-judicial opinion should be given . . . in any case? Is your tribunal organized to exhaust its time in dissertation on ordinary subjects of political speculation? To decide upon the merits of any cause without jurisdiction to entertain it (is) contrary to all law, precedent and principle.

After *McCulloch v. Maryland,* in which the Court decided that Maryland could not tax the United States Bank, the South and the West lashed out at the Court for failing to strike down an act of Congress. The criticism was voiced in a manner mindful of the assaults upon the Court after *Marbury v. Madison,* although it was then directed against a totally contradictory decision. Ohio even refused to accept the McCulloch decision and forcibly seized money from the Ohio branch of the United States Bank to cover the state taxes the Supreme Court had declared unconstitutional. Federal marshals had to unscramble that one.

Most people have forgotten the attacks against the Court from the North after Chief Justice Taney's opinion in the Dred Scott Case, which ruled that Congress had no right to exclude slavery from the territories. The North's *Atlantic Monthly* in protest wrote: ". . . The most sacred and blinding compacts of former years, were annulled to make way for it; and the judicial department of the government was violently hauled from its sacred retreat, into the political arena, to give the gratuitous *coup-de-grâce* to the old opinions and the apparent sanction of law to the new dogma." And in a later issue: "Whatever the . . . judges of the Supreme Court may seek to maintain, they cannot upset the universal logic of the law, nor extinguish the fundamental principles of our political system."

Denunciations of this sort were followed by plans and proposals to clip the Court's wings. Few foresaw that it would take a civil war to reverse *Dred Scott*. An error, no matter how basic, is not cured by abolishing or crippling the constitutional institution whence it came.

The consternation over some of the decisions of the Supreme Court in the area of national security was possibly insignificant compared to some of these more ancient battles that the Court has survived.

History, common sense, instinct, and a small knowledge of the fallibility of systems, programs, and organizations all tell me that those decisions of the Supreme Court deciding the case on the side of the individual were sound decisions and that the Court properly exercised its legitimate powers in deciding them as it did. It misses the point to argue that these decisions and opinions gave aid and comfort to those who would undo us. The function of the Court is not to oppose those who would overthrow us; it is to apply constitutional and legal principles to specific cases. It is even more absurd to attack the Court because of these decisions on the ground that the Court has overreached its powers. Even if one were tempted to call those decisions political moralizing they can hardly be said to have broken new frontiers—they only brought us back to a level of sanity which this country had not experienced for a period of time, caught up as it was in a frenzy of fear out of all proportion to the facts. "Such fears as these," Learned Hand tells us, "are a solvent which can eat out the cement that binds the stones together."

There will always be disagreement with the work of the Supreme Court. The Court does not labor in a vacuum. We may support the Court's conclusions, or we may oppose them. We are secure in our right to approve decisions of the Court only insofar as others are secure in their right to criticize them. There is a difference between criticism and ignoble attack in this instance, for the Supreme Court is a naked institution. The Constitution has provided it with no means of enforcing its decisions; its effectiveness as an institution and as a constituent element of our system of government rests entirely upon the voluntary acceptance of its decrees by other elements of government and by the people. Disagreement with the Court's decrees will not enfeeble its institutional strength. But disagreement coupled with broadside attacks upon the institution itself or upon the character or purpose of the Justices will surely erode the institution at its base.

Particularly in times of stress, we cannot risk the loosening of our strongest bulwark against any enemy, that defeats the fundamental liberties embodied in our Constitution. Without a strong and independent Judiciary the weakening of both our individual liberties and our national security surely will result.

7

The Alliance with the Old World

For several years I was a member of the United States Congressional delegation to the North Atlantic Treaty Organization Parliamentarians Conference, last serving as Chairman of the Political Committee of the Conference. The latter office, Chairman of the Political Committee, was particularly gratifying to me, because it was by election of the European members.

The assignment took me to Europe for brief trips two or three times a year, and our subject during these conferences was the future of the Atlantic Alliance.

Possibly the most valuable aspect of these meetings, from my own point of view at least, was the knowledge I gained from the friendships formed with members of other Parliaments.

We quickly discover that we have mutual problems, common aspirations, and interchangeable practices. Often among parliamentarians there is a frankness and a respect that one never seems to discover among the statesmen and ministers in their diplomatic dealings with each other. Members of Congress and members of parliaments fully and quickly recognize the need for discussion and debate, for reasonable compromises, for resolutions of inflammatory situations, and for new discoveries and common agreements for the future. The men and women who are the instruments of free elections understand the importance of government being subject to the will of the people.

The Atlantic community has been beset by troubles, one of them being the obduracy of the French Government in excluding the British from the Common Market, in its independence of NATO, and in moving to develop a separate independent nuclear weapons capability. There is a growing question among European leaders and students of government in this country of the efficacy of parliamentary institutions in general as presently constituted in the new age. Increasingly one sees reference to the need for a strengthening of parliamentary systems. There is a growing awareness of the problem of individual members of Congress and parliaments in staying abreast of (much less on top of) the complexities of the scientific age in which we live. And to some extent we are beginning to see the revolt of the back-benchers, the little-heard-from junior members of parliaments who are demanding a greater voice in the councils of state.

There is a need for communication. Despite common objectives, there is misunderstanding in our relations with our Western European allies. The kind of unity needed for a partnership of equals and our outdated present conception of a weak, dependent, and compliant Europe are incompatible. The strong and prosperous Europe which has emerged largely as a result of farsighted American policies after World War II now demands a role in the Alliance in keeping with its new strength. With only one exception, the leaders of the new Europe—and their peoples as well, I believe—do not wish to exclude American influence from Europe; on the contrary, they wish to invest further in our Alliance, not as clients but as equal partners.

The United States is committed in theory to a partnership of equals with its European allies. In practice, however, serious errors of judgment have been made, indicating a continuing recalcitrance on our part. One such error which had serious consequences was the sudden withdrawal of American support for Britain's Skybolt program in 1962, which was first announced at the Nassau conference between Prime Minister Macmillan and President Kennedy, which, in turn, heightened General de Gaulle's suspicions of the "Anglo-Saxons" and probably contributed to his decision to exclude Britain from the European Economic Community. Another blunder was our insistence on a European Defense Community in the face of intense French opposition, a stand which ultimately destroyed the project and greatly embarrassed the United States. The example of the EDC is relevant because there are indications that a harsh and insensitive

American policy may bring on a similar fate for any possible solution of the haunting, unsolved problem of the control of nuclear weapons production and usage in Europe.

My experience leads me to believe that we should consult our allies more; better yet, let us give them their full due and deal with them. We have not yet, for example, really dealt with de Gaulle and his conception of a United Europe; we have tended to ignore him or placate him. Unless the allies can work things out as equals, de Gaulle's plan for Europe may come to have an appeal for Europeans which it could never earn on its own merits.

Beyond these difficulties lies the need for a total strengthening—not a weakening—of the Atlantic community. Long-term military alliances have a way of hardening and becoming inflexible. Lasting alliances must be based on deeper ties, engaging more positive human values. The Atlantic nations must be welded together by the dynamism of free systems working together toward peaceful and progressive goals. Imperialistic Communism can never compete with free economies, free political, social, scientific, and cultural institutions working together for the advancement of the well-being of mankind.

The weakening of NATO and of the Atlantic Alliance is part of the new nationalism that has mushroomed throughout the world—in Europe, in Asia, Africa, Latin America, and in the United States as well. And history begins to repeat itself in the new struggle between East and West. The question is whether we can live with these conflicts by designing a world rule of law administered by international institutions. That is the main challenge. What we must do is just the opposite of what the virus of nationalism tempts us to do, which is to break down lines of communication, to erect barriers, and to escalate hostilities. The proper prescription is the strengthening of international institutions such as the United Nations and the development of world peace through a world rule of law. The old game of power politics, of coalition, of threat and counterthreat among nations has never been able to solve the problem of war and peace. It is all the more essential in the age of the hydrogen bomb that international institutions be strengthened and new ones constructed where necessary to avoid a repetition of history.

The NATO Parliamentarians Conference is now called the North Atlantic Assembly. Each year it meets in plenary session usually in Europe, preceded by meetings of its several committees. It is an informal body, without status of powers, consisting of members of parliaments and Congress of the NATO nations. Originally it confined itself to military and politico-military matters, NATO being a military alliance. In later years the Conference broadened its field of discussion to include economic, social, scientific, and cultural affairs. The work of its Political Committee, of which I had been the Rapporteur (or Secretary) for several years before becoming Chairman, increasingly has moved into areas of political concern to all Atlantic countries, as well as NATO. The Common Market and the economy of Europe have played a greater role. The political problems growing out of economic, scientific, and military advances of all Atlantic nations have become more acute.

In 1962 the Political Committee issued a report which suggested the creation of an Atlantic Assembly that would have a measure of power and that would have among its membership all the free countries of the Atlantic community. The report pointed out that there is no common parliamentary body cognizant of all Atlantic institutions by which the peoples of the nations involved may be represented directly. It argued that two assemblies and two only are in fact needed, namely a European parliament (which already exists) and an Atlantic Assembly. It concluded that these should evolve by the development of the existing institutions. We said: "Only by the establishment of a wide, strong, parliamentary body, provided with access to needed information and empowered to provide the executive bodies, not merely of NATO, not merely of OECD, but of all Atlantic institutions, only so may the energies of the separate national democracies be directed to more common goals under a system of open debate and popular representation. Only so may those common goals be achieved with due regard for uncommon heritages and national liberties."

A consultative Atlantic Assembly, properly constituted, would be a common meeting place for parliamentarians of all free Atlantic countries. It would have the right to ask questions and receive answers for executive branch diplomats. It would recommend and consult. It would not have the power to force policy in executive branch institutions, but the public impact of new policy statements would be substantial. Finally, it would provide the vehicle for softening the tensions that develop in the interchange of ideas and viewpoints among friendly nations.

8

The Old Age of Aid

ONE OF the greatest sources of frustrations to many members of Congress is the annual debate over foreign aid.

It usually is a very bad debate, full of superficialities and platitudes. The main heat often is generated over irrelevancies, and the subject itself is entangled in as many conflicts and contradictions as the ordinary condition of the world.

Indeed, if the world were not in a state of general upheaval and change, there would be no discussion of foreign aid; no one would need it.

For twenty years the American people have helped others by projects ranging from the reconstruction of the European economies left shattered by World War II to the introduction of basic health and educational facilities in developing countries. Throughout the period we have debated among ourselves the real and alleged shortcomings of our aid and whether we ought to have an aid program at all.

It is true that foreign aid has not fulfilled the hopes with which we undertook it, but that has more to do with the extravagance of our hopes than with the failures of our aid. The value of foreign aid in the past is not open to serious challenge. The Marshall Plan saved Europe from Communist domination after World War II and set it on the road to its current prosperity. Our aid also has been effective in the much more difficult task of contributing to economic growth in the less developed nations of Asia, Africa, and Latin America. According to the calculations of Dr. Isaiah Frank of Johns Hopkins University, economic growth in the less developed world since 1950 has been at the impressive rate of 4.2 percent a year. A per capita growth rate of about 2 percent has been achieved, the rapid increase in population notwithstanding.

Greece, Israel, and Taiwan have all developed strong economies with the assistance of American aid. India has made steady if unobtrusive progress while maintaining a functioning democracy among a population which is over a third that of the entire underdeveloped world. Western aid in the form of foreign exchange and surplus food has substantially helped Pakistan and India, taken together, to maintain an annual industrial growth rate of about 8 percent. In Africa, where development is hampered by a lack of skills of all kinds, Western aid is bringing about an educational revolution.

The Alliance for Progress has now, despite shortcomings of administration and other difficulties, achieved a limited measure of success. Statistics for 1964, for example, showed an average increase of per capita income in Latin America of 3 percent, a sizable part of which may in fact have been the result of our aid program. The construction of dwelling units and schoolrooms, roads, some new industries, new hospitals, somewhat increased food production, and expanded business activity have generated some new attitudes and the beginnings of commitments to social and economic reforms in several of the Latin American republics. Again, some of this has been made possible by our country's efforts.

In most of the less developed nations, whether they are under democratic government or military rule or some form of home-grown socialism, there has been no demonstrable rush toward Communism. In a few of these areas, Communist proselytizing has ceased to be an important threat.

When all the revolutions of the twentieth century—national, ideological, military, and economic—are assessed in the perspective of history, it is not unlikely that the revolution of economic development will be judged the most important. Prior to World War II rapid economic development was almost a purely Western achievement. In the last twenty years it has become global, and it is changing the face of societies that have been economically stagnant for centuries. With a growth rate of a little over 4 percent a year, the total income of the underdeveloped world has about doubled in the last fifteen to twenty years. A revolution consequently is being wrought in the lives of the great majority of the world's population and, like all revolutions, it carries both the promise of a better life and the certainty of untimely disappointments and profound dislocations.

In the foreseeable future, the world economic revolution is likely to generate many more problems than it will solve. One problem is the unevenness of economic development, not only among countries but within the various sectors of national economies. Specifically, in many underdeveloped countries industrial growth proceeds at a satisfactory rate while agriculture lags far behind—so much so that in some countries agricultural production per capita is less than it was ten or fifteen years ago. At best, food production the world over is barely keeping pace with population growth.

Another critical problem is trade. In the last twenty years world trade has expanded at an unprecedented rate, but most of the expansion has taken place in trade among the advanced countries and in exports from the advanced to the less developed countries. Exports from the poorer countries, chiefly primary products, have not risen greatly. As a result, these nations are unable to earn the foreign exchange necessary to finance their development. To some extent, this is attributable to neglect of export industries by the underdeveloped countries; the most important reason is simply that they are in the wrong businesses, exporting primary products such as basic foodstuffs and industrial raw materials for which demand rises very slowly. The unrewarding result has been a continuous decline in the prices of commodities exported by the less developed countries and increasingly higher prices of products imported from advanced nations. The deterioration of the terms of trade thus threatens to choke off economic development unless the advanced nations provide a steady and adequate flow of essential foreign exchange.

Another problem arising from the slow growth of export earnings is a mounting burden of foreign debts. Many less developed countries are so heavily burdened with short-term debts that an alarmingly high proportion of their future export earnings—in some cases up to 25 or 30 percent—is pledged to debt service over the next few years. Many American cities, I am sad to note are similarly trammeled.

There are great threats to the continued economic development of industrially weak countries. First, they may be compelled to forego necessary imports to service their debts. Second, they cannot afford, and lenders are unlikely to provide, further loans at conventional rates of interest.

Overriding all the other threats to economic development is the population increase. At the current rate, the world population will double in the next forty years. Most of the increase will occur in the underdeveloped countries. To maintain even their existing levels of nutrition, housing, health, and education, the poorer nations will have to double their production in the next forty years. About two-thirds of all their potential new investment will be devoted not to raising those levels, but to meeting the needs of increased population. Unless the growth of population is brought under control, it is unlikely that even the most intelligent development programs will be able to achieve and sustain acceptable living standards.

The scope of the development problem and our own vital

interest in it answers the question of whether American involvement in the business of aid has run its course.

It has not, even though its form may, and should, be changed. The stability it has helped to create is still tenuous and may remain so for a long, long time. Without stability in large portions of the globe, our own system is threatened.

Once the need for stability is understood, we can turn to more pertinent questions. What kind of aid is most needed? By whom? How can we make our aid as efficient and productive as possible? How can we improve our own bilateral aid program? Most importantly, to what extent, and in what ways, can we cooperate with other nations to provide economic aid through multilateral channels, converting it from a national charity to an international responsibility?

I believe that the most important single contribution the United States could make to the success of the development century would be the multilateralization of most of our economic assistance. Our development loans—that part of our aid which finances basic industrial and economic development as distinguished from military assistance and other forms of aid designed to serve short-term political purposes —should be diverted from bilateral management by the Agency for International Development to multilateral management by the World Bank's International Development Association.

Three major purposes would be served by channeling our development aid through IDA: First, it will establish economic development as an essential objective in itself, to be promoted by an agency with no political goals except the development of the world's poorer nations; second, it will largely remove economic aid from the mounting pressures of our own domestic politics; third, it will begin to convert the assistance of the rich nations to the poor nations from separate acts of generosity to something closer to a community responsibility.

Far from being a major departure in American foreign policy, the internationalization of aid represents a logical transition in the United States' ventures in world order. Internationalism became a major force in world affairs after the First World War. The League of Nations soon foundered, but the World Court survived and the International Labor Organization, which was created along with the League, not only survived but has come to exert important influence on labor laws, working conditions, and industrial relations in many countries. The League itself had some limited political successes and some notable successes in the social and economic field.

From these cautious, occasionally productive ventures in world order, the idea began to take hold that communities of national effort towards peace made more sense than unbridled nationalism. It became unmistakably clear in World War II that the United States would be required to take a leading role in building international institutions.

After World War II, the United States committed itself to military and diplomatic international cooperation. But we have not yet shown a commensurate willingness to unite our efforts with those of other nations in the equally important field of social and economic cooperation with the world's less developed nations. We have done a good deal toward making the United Nations an effective multinational instrument for keeping the peace, although recently our government has shown signs of wearying in this effort, and more persevering leadership is required. We have committed ourselves to multinational defense alliances such as NATO and the Organization of American States, although here too there has been an unfortunate deterioration of United States leadership. But in the field of social and economic assistance we have clung tenaciously to an outmoded bilateralism.

The institutions for international cooperation in aid already exist. The World Bank is a solid success and its "soft loan" affiliate, the International Development Association, is a going concern, as is the Inter-American Development Bank. We have only to decide to make full use of their facilities. This decision in turn depends on our willingness to make a fundamental commitment to the idea that we are living in the development century, and that the United States has a direct stake in the development of areas undergoing change.

The International Development Association was formed in 1960 as an affiliate of the World Bank to provide funds for essential projects that developing countries could not finance by conventional loans. The IDA, which is under the same management and staff as the Bank, extends fifty-year, no-interest credits bearing an annual service charge of ¾ of one percent. By July 1966, IDA had extended 89 credits amounting to almost $1.4 billion to 32 countries in Asia,

Africa, Europe, and Latin America for such purposes as transportation, agriculture, industrial development, power, telecommunications, water supplies, and education.

I believe it would be a great advance for American interests, for the development of the poorer nations, and for the broader purpose of building a world community if the United States were to channel much or most of its development lending through such international agencies as IDA and the Inter-American Development Bank. Having taken the lead over the last twenty years in efforts to build an international security community, the United States should now take the lead in building a no less important community for social and economic development.

As the Republican Citizens' Critical Issues Council pointed out, in a remarkably good paper, aid channeled through international agencies can often achieve American objectives (long-term objectives, it should be added, not short-term manipulations) better than direct United States aid. "It has been learned from experience," said the Council, "that frequently there is less resentment and resistance from an underdeveloped nation when the World Bank, for example, rather than AID, conditions a loan on a specific government concession to private enterprise."

A profound psychological problem is involved in bilateral aid, although it does not affect an international agency such as the World Bank. Bilateral loans carry an inevitable connotation of charity which, put in the worst light, has an element of humiliation for the borrower and irritation or embarrassment for the lender. Neither can ever quite forget that one is in need, the other without material need. Human nature being what it is, this is not the kind of relationship that imparts self-confidence or self-sufficiency to the borrower or generosity and tolerance to the lender. Genuinely grateful though he may be, the borrower eventually will resent his benefactor because he is rich. The lender, in turn, may become exasperated with the borrower because he is needy, in some ways inefficient, and ungrateful besides.

There has been a great deal of talk about ingratitude for our aid, and it is well to put the matter in perspective. Effusive gratitude is contrary to human nature. The United States, for example, was not overly appreciative to France for helping us win our Revolution in 1783; in fact, we almost went to war with France a few years later. Nor did the halls of Congress ring with gratitude to England during the century that the British fleet provided us with free security from the power politics of Europe; on the contrary, the nineteenth century was a period of most eloquent and outspoken Anglophobia in America. The point is that thankfulness is an unrealistic objective of foreign policy and a most unworthy objective for a great nation. "Magnanimity in politics," said Edmund Burke, "is not seldom the truest wisdom; and a great empire and little minds go ill together."

Bilateral aid has been described as an instrument for influencing the policies of recipient countries. In many instances, our aid has given us temporary leverage, although often at the cost of ingrained resentments on the part of nationalist leaders. The belief that aid gives us direct and immediate influence on the behavior of its beneficiaries is belied by our experiences. The United States provided massive assistance to the Republic of Korea and fought a war to defend its independence. When the peace negotiations reached a decisive state in 1953, the government of President Syngman Rhee attempted to abort them. The United States provided billions of dollars to revive France after World War II, and now a fully recovered France is creating difficulties for American policy all over the world.

The political usage of aid also has been appraised by the Republican Critical Issues Council: "It is imperative," the Council wrote, "that we distinguish clearly between hostility and mere differences of opinion, or even sharp clashes of view on particular matters. . . . The country's direction must be clear; but, in pursuing basic objectives on which there is agreement, differences in judgment will always be found on individual points of foreign policy. Moreover, our own judgment may not always be right. Besides, we stand for independence, and in exercising independence countries must be free to seek their own way through the perplexities of today's situations, in a manner they believe serves their own interests. We are trying to build free nations, not to make satellites. It is Communism that demands subservience."

The decisive advantage of the international lending agencies is their economic objectivity and the fact that this objectivity is well known to both contributors and borrowers. As Eugene R. Black has put it: "Economic priorities are inevitably confused when economic objectivity is lost—and economic objectivity is not easy when aid is influenced by political ends. . . . The Bank, and IDA, for example, can apply what should be the real criterion—the practical merits of the particular case. Because they are known to have no ulterior motive, they can exert more influence over the use of a loan than is possible for a bilateral lender. They can insist that the projects for which they lend are established on a sound basis, and—most important—they can make their lending conditional upon commensurate efforts by the recipient country itself."

Even if our development lending were channeled entirely through the international lending agencies, some of our foreign aid would necessarily remain bilateral—military assistance, stopgap budgetary support, and all the various forms of assistance that have short-term political aims as distinguished from long-range economic objectives. Broadly speaking, the division of aid between bilateral military and political assistance and multilateral development assistance reflects the reality of a world which, though still divided by national and ideological rivalries, is struggling slowly and painfully toward the creation of a broader community.

The distinction between the two kinds of foreign aid is of the greatest importance. In the words of a statement issued by some fifty American development experts:

This generation lies between two worlds; an old world in which sovereign national states regard each other as allies or enemies; and a new world, still adolescent, in which nation states recognize their interdependence and engage cooperatively in the tasks of mutual benefit and concern.

What is commonly called "foreign aid" is a mixture of governmental measures appropriate to the old world and of others quite different that are appropriate to the new. Military aid and short-term politically motivated economic aid . . . could suffice to the old world. Developmental assistance . . . is an essential additional activity of the new world of increasingly interdependent states.

The multilateralization of development lending is the most important reform needed in our foreign aid. There also is need for improvement, however, in the conduct of the programs that would remain bilateral should our development lending be internationalized. A most desirable reform in this category would be a continuing review of both country programs and the bilateral aid program as a whole by nongovernmental economists and technical experts. The participants in the periodic reviews should be wholly independent, engaged by the government solely for the purpose of surveying the conduct of aid, documenting both its successes and shortcomings, and providing objective information to the Congress and the public.

There is a need for greater selectivity in our aid. What has been achieved thus far is concentration rather than selectivity. The President pointed out in his foreign aid message of January 14, 1965, that 64 percent of our development aid went to only seven countries in fiscal year 1964; he did not point out that we nonetheless maintain aid programs of one sort or another in about ninety countries. Many of these are designed to do nothing more than maintain an American "presence"—an irritating and purposeless presence, in some instances, the elimination of which might very well lead to better relations with the countries concerned.

A final and most important need is public education. It would be useful and constructive if the Administration were to undertake a sustained effort to inform the American people quite candidly as to what can and cannot be expected of foreign aid and why it should be regarded not as something abnormal but as an instrument of policy in this development century. As the Critical Issues Council points out, the resolution of the controversy over aid ultimately depends on the quality of political leadership exerted in its behalf. "Aid," they write, "has few constituents, and few politicians ready to fight for it. More important, there are few ready to educate for it. A wide, sustained, educational effort should be promoted to bring the aid story to more people."

Such an educational effort should seek, above all, to remind Americans of both the challenge and the promise of foreign aid. The challenge is to our enlightened self-interest and to a necessary and decent concern with the stability of other areas; the promise is hope for emerging peoples and a measure of stability for established peoples in a world struggling through change and looking hopefully, though at times despairingly, for peace.

9

The United States and the Movement of People

We are, perhaps more than any country, a nation of immigrants. People of all lands—more than forty-one million of them—established, sustained, and fulfilled the United States. All aspects of our national life—politics, religion, commerce, and the arts—have been molded by this, the greatest folk-migration in history. America has done much for the immigrant. The immigrant has done even more for America.

Yet until passage of the 1965 Immigration and Nationality Act reforms, we adhered to a senseless and blatantly discriminatory immigration policy that evaluated human beings not on the basis of what they are, but where they were born. Our policy resembled a national real estate covenant. We preferred not to discuss it unless it was threatened.

In Congress, as a member of the Committee with jurisdiction over immigration policy, I always raised this issue with some trepidation, for it had been a popular but erroneous belief that reform of the immigration laws would throw open the United States to a flood of undesirables.

I often thought of Mr. Dooley's observation:

"As a pilgrim father that missed the first boats," said Mr. Dooley, "I must raise me clarion voice agin the invasion of this fair land by the paupers and anarchists of effete Europe. Ye bet I must—because I'm here first."

Almost no one has seriously suggested that we permit unlimited immigration. We cannot now return to the open-door policies of a less complex age. To promise entry to all who wish to come here would create insurmountable problems for the United States and would do little to solve the problems of the countries from which the immigrants came. Our friends abroad certainly understand our position.

Our immigration policy must conform with our capacity to absorb; common sense makes it so. But the practice of restricting immigration by placing quotas on individual nations was both illogical and unconscionable. The national origins system reflected a sad and unnecessary conflict with our national ideals. As long as the quota system was based on national origins it was a source of pain and of shame. With the Act of 1965, signed by the President on Ellis Island, the system was substantially corrected. The redress was salutary; not only because the quota system was parochial and inequitous, but because it was the atavistic symbol of an attitude this country had outgrown.

Our immigration laws have an interesting history.

The young United States had a very liberal immigration policy. We proclaimed the principle that a religious test would not be required for public officeholders; we held every public office in the country—with the exception of the Presidency itself—open to naturalized citizens. Both policies were established primarily to stimulate immigration.

Many laws enacted since that time have either set or retained limitations on immigration. The first were the Oriental Exclusion Acts, originally passed in 1882, which placed a flat ban on the Chinese and Japanese. In 1917, over President Woodrow Wilson's veto, the Congress created the Asiatic Barred Zone, which was the forerunner of the national origins system. It excluded persons from India, Burma, Siam, and other countries located in what came to be called the "Asia-Pacific Triangle."

With these exceptions, our immigration laws were qualitative; that is, they excluded only those persons who failed to pass certain minimal tests of health, literacy, and good conduct. The quota law of 1921 and the Johnson-Reed Immigration Act of 1924 changed all that.

The Johnson-Reed Act limited the total number of immigrants who could enter the United States in any one year to 150,000. The Act also provided that the annual quota for any nationality should bear the same ratio to 150,000 as the number of persons of that nationality in this country bore to the total population of the United States. The most recent census, in 1920, was taken as the base for determining nationality population ratios. "Descendants of slaves"—in other words, virtually the entire Negro population of the United States—were not counted in computing the ratios. The purpose of the Act was to freeze the then-existing national structure of the American population.

The year following passage of the Act, total immigration to the United States fell from 706,896 to 294,314. Although immigrations continued at about that level until the early nineteen-thirties, it has been only since 1950 that the figure has consistently exceeded 200,000.

The most important single revision of our immigration laws was the Immigration and Nationality Act, commonly known as the McCarran-Walter Act, which was enacted over President Truman's veto in 1952. The Act attempted to codify the plethora of laws, amendments, regulations, proclamations, executive orders, rules, operational instructions, clarifications, dispensations, and circumventions that had grown up around the Johnson-Reed Act over the years. Indeed, the Act made a number of worthwhile changes: It eliminated discrimination between the sexes and gave preferential status to skilled aliens; it repealed the Oriental Exclusion Acts by setting token quotas for nations in the Asia-Pacific Triangle; it gave Asian spouses and the children of American citizens nonquota status; it eliminated race as a bar to naturalization.

But it did not abrogate the humiliating racial philosophy by which we overtly discriminated against more than one-half of the world's population; the national origins quota system emerged intact.

It was not until 1965 that Congress finally endorsed abolition of the national origins system and reformed other anachronistic segments of the McCarran-Walter Act.

The ultimate objective of the new law is to create a world-wide pool, without a country-of-origin distinction, from which immigrants would be chosen on a first-come, first-served basis. However, aliens with relatives here or with skills valuable to this country, would be given preferential assignment of numbers quota. I should add that the preferences would use up most of the quota, leaving very few quota numbers for nonpreference categories.

Mere numbers are not the problem. I was concerned in Congress not with statistics, but with a philosophy. My objective, and that of others like Congressman Emanuel Celler who pressed for change, was to give the country an honorable policy with which to govern our immigration and to move toward the total abandonment of the national origins system. The Act of 1965 was a major step toward this goal.

The Act also took up another area that needed attention and in which I had long had an active interest. This was the plight of refugees and escapees from Communist-dominated countries. Of all immigration problems, one of the most explosive and tragic has been posed by refugees.

According to the most reliable evidence available, up to ten million unsettled persons have lived outside the Iron Curtain. In the years since World War II over forty million human beings have been involuntarily uprooted from their homes and have crossed frontiers, artificial or traditional, in search of asylum. The tragic proliferation of refugees all over the world is one of the legacies of an era of global wars, revolutions, civil conflicts, and surging nationalist movements.

Refugees are both the product of political tensions and the cause of new unrest. Wherever there is an unsolved refugee problem, there is both a tragic human situation and a potentially explosive political situation. When refugee problems are neglected—as they all too often have been—human misery abounds and political tensions are aggravated.

In the autumn of 1956 I served along with General Joseph Swing as the representative of Attorney General Herbert Brownell in Austria and West Germany in setting up the machinery under which almost forty thousand refugees from Communist tyranny in Hungary were brought into the United States. Many an early dawn we stood on the Austrian side of the bridge at Andau. We saw courageous freedom fighters, women and children with them, cross the freezing swamps and canals to reach sanctuary beyond the Hungarian border. It was a sight and experience that I shall never forget. Anyone who has witnessed the chaos, the fear, the suffering of human beings in mass flight from their homeland can never again think of the plight of uprooted peoples as anything less than an urgent and compelling demand on individual conscience and human compassion.

Four years later, as a member of the Committee of the Congress writing the refugee laws of our country, I had the opportunity in the course of a world tour of refugee camps to study the living history of four significant concentrations of refugees: Arabs in the territories around Israel, Tibetans in India, both Muslim and Hindu refugees in India and Pakistan, and Chinese in Hong Kong.

In crowded, wretched camps—in bitterness and often in deprivation—children and adults, existed without hope in a world they could not understand, without the conditions of human dignity which we Americans have come to accept as a basic part of our birthright.

One of the most interesting parts of that trip was a visit I made with a State Department aide to the foothills of the Himalayas in the north of India, near the borders of Nepal and Tibet, to see the Dalai Lama, exiled ruler of Tibet. We traveled by plane, train, and truck, from hot to cold weather, low altitudes to high. Being among the first Americans in any official capacity to talk with the Dalai Lama, we found the experience rewarding and unforgettable. We learned much. The refugee problem was, of course, tragic and without immediate solution. Tibetans feared dispersion, a fear born of an intense desire to hold together their religious and cultural institutions, and yet in the area of Dharamsala, where the Indian government had confined the Tibetan refugee population, there was little work. At the same time, the altitude and cool weather were desirable for health— even if the Tibetan refugees could have been absorbed into the Indian lowlands, the heat would have been injurious to them. The Dalai Lama was chiefly interested in education for his younger men. Obviously this resettlement problem had to be handled on almost a one-by-one basis—carefully and selectively.

To any refugee problem there are three possible solutions:

repatriation in the country of origin, integration in the country of asylum, or resettlement elsewhere. Some combination of integration, resettlement, and repatriation is essential in meeting all refugee problems.

In suggesting lines of action to alleviate the world refugee problems, we should, wherever possible, encourage programs of relief and rehabilitation under the auspices of the United Nations and through the machinery and resources of the International Committee on European Migration (ICEM), which has done excellent work with European migration problems. The United Nations and ICEM should expand their mandates to encompass all world refugee problems instead of limiting themselves to the declining problem of Europe.

Voluntary agencies have done remarkable work in each of these areas. They have accomplished miracles in the distribution of food and supplies, transportation and relocation. Congressional legislation passed in 1962 enabled the United States to continue its participation in certain refugee programs to provide assistance to refugees after their arrival in the United States. It authorized the President to use up to ten million dollars to meet unexpected refugee developments which are outside the scope of regular appropriations.

The new law of 1965 provided a more basic humanization of our official stance toward the homeless of the world. It was wise that it did so, for the refugee problem should be considered as an integral part of over-all immigration policy, and of foreign policy as well.

10

The Why of Politics

POLITICS is said to be a dirty word in the United States, and too often it is. But politics and government are twins; one doesn't exist or function without the other. It is banal, but nonetheless true, that politics and government are only as good as the people would have them. If politics is a dirty word, and if we have inferior politicians, those who passively complain about them are as much at fault as anyone.

Yet the terrible need for competence, caliber, and character in politics is manifest. Free institutions are constantly changing and sometimes are threatened. But free institutions as we know and accept them are maintained only through politics. I am reminded of the square-jawed masters of ceremony at hotel dinners who believe they compliment the politician by separating him from the pack and calling him a statesman. Our greatest statesmen were statesmen only because they were master politicians. Abraham Lincoln was a thorough-going politician, as were both Roose-velts, Theodore and Franklin.

In English political history, Benjamin Disraeli was also a great conservative party Prime Minister because he was a master politician. The same is true of the Pitts, Gladstone, Lloyd George, and Winston Churchill. In Israel there was, and still is, Ben-Gurion; in India, there were Gandhi and Nehru. Thought of by the world at large as statesmen, which they were indeed, they were also highly intelligent and shrewd politicians first and last. They ran hard for office, they knew the importance of political organization, they understood the necessity for fence-mending and daily political chores. They knew when to stand and when to yield. As politico-statesmen they understood a definition of statesmanship once given by Edmund Burke: "Well to know the right time and manner of yielding that which it is impossible to keep."

I have watched the workings of the free democratic process in a great many countries—from the United States to Europe, the Middle East, and the Far East. Wherever I examined the process at work, I came away impressed with the likeness of people. Politics in free governments is essentially alike the world over. Members of Parliament in countries such as England, Ireland, Canada, France, Belgium, Holland, Italy, Israel, and India follow the same practices as those in the United States. They caucus, they hold meetings, they make stump speeches and promises, kiss babies and march in parades. In any country where men and women in public office live or die politically by the ballot box the competition is similar. This is the essense of free government. As

long as it continues, as long as people remember that freedom and competitive political endeavor are inseparable,
then free institutions will prevail.

It is interesting to compare parliamentary institutions in
different countries. As a Congressman, I enjoyed immensely
exchanging informative tidbits with members of various
parliaments and representative bodies—their practices and
habits, their means of communication, and their availability
to their constituents.

Probably the members of the United States Congress stay
closer to the people, their constituents, than any other representatives of legislative bodies around the world that I know
of.

There is much that we can learn from other, often much
older, systems. But on the question of a representative's
relations with his people, others have been learning from us.
Members of foreign parliaments who come to the United
States to observe, invariably are amazed at the general availability of a Congressman to his constituents. Increasingly
they adopt our technique in this regard, as they have also
tended to adopt our campaign techniques.

I suspect that the Congressman's availability is one prime
reason why our Federal system has worked as well as it has
over the years. Certainly, I found it one of the most enjoyable and useful parts of the job. On weekends, while Congress was in session, I would return to New York City and
spend part of Friday or Saturday in the small District office
at 30 West Forty-fourth Street that I opened after I was first
elected. There I held constituent "clinics" to diagnose the

problems people brought in. Sometimes, like a doctor, I was able to prescribe cures. Suggestions also were presented, and on some occasions they found their way into the governmental stream. My office, in brief, allowed people to participate directly in their government, by talking to their elected representative.

I believe that this practice, followed as it is by most Congressmen, softens the arbitrariness and hardness of big government and shrinks its remoteness.

There were many other satisfactions in being a Congressman. These overcame moments of frustration when I wondered why I was not back in my old profession trying cases in the courts.

Every member of Congress will tell you that there is no headier satisfaction than winning a point of debate on the floor of the House or Senate. When a member carries his point to final conclusion by winning a close vote on an amendment he has offered, he is divertingly happy; he forgets all the petty annoyances and harassments that troubled him a day earlier.

Most legislators, in short, enjoy legislating. Despite the frustrations of the legislative process, I found it immensely absorbing to draft a bill and see it through the tortuous pathways of the Congress. For example, shortly after I became a member I originated legislation to reorganize the procedures under which sponsors were chosen for Title I housing projects under The National Housing Act. Title I of the Act was used most often for middle income housing—privately sponsored, but assisted by land write-downs. In New York City,

serious problems began to develop when a few middle income projects turned into high income housing, and the
identity of the real owners was discovered to have been hid-
den. I drafted legislation to compel public identification of
project sponsors, introduced it, and began the long quest for
support in and out of the Congress. Support came from New
York City, with the notable exception of Robert Moses, who
at the time was controlling the Title I housing programs out
of the offices of the Triborough Bridge and Tunnel Authority. The Federal Urban Renewal Administration withheld
comment. When the omnibus housing bill came to the floor
of the House, I offered my bill as an amendment. After a
brief debate, the amendment was accepted. A good deal of
personal diplomacy was devoted to steering it through the
Senate, and it became law.

As a member of the Judiciary Committee in the House of
Representatives, I drafted bill after bill on civil rights, and
offered many amendments to those drafted by others. I was
fortunate to play a role, from beginning to end, in the making of three historic civil rights bills.

Seeing language from its beginning stages to final law,
hammered about by discussion and debate, is an experience
almost uniquely enjoyed by lawyers and legislators. Both
law and politics have the possibility of bringing about justice
where there was injustice; it is the noblest aspect of both
professions.

During the years I was a member of Congress, I devoted
as much time as I could to the universities, colleges, and
high schools of my district and, as I add it up, to a surprising

number of universities across the country. I lectured, took seminars, and spent days "in residence" as a visiting fellow. I did it for several reasons. First, I enjoyed it. Second, I learned a good deal that I found helpful in my work (I have regularly used college interns in my government offices). Third, Republican officeholders ought to be seen and heard more frequently on the campus.

The question asked of me most frequently by students (usually privately) is: "How should I go about getting into politics?" I would guess that it is the number one question asked of most men in politics by students. I always am pleased when the question is presented; it compensates for the view that many others form of the profession. But I wish I could give more precise answers to the question.

I have suggested to the inquiring student that he hold to his ambition. As long as he has it and is willing to work and experiment, it may be fulfilled. But he must remember that many will try to dissuade him from entering the political lists. Most important, I suggest that he advance his education, wherever and however he can, as far as he can. A postgraduate degree helps, not necessarily in law as many think, but in the field where his interest is most intense. The important requirement is acquiring the mental discipline essential to a successful career in any field. There is no sure road and there are no certain charts. In politics every formula that has been made has ultimately been broken. Politics is more an art than a science. Hence its capacity for newness and change is greater than is generally thought. It requires men and women who, in addition to having achieved technical knowledge, have trained themselves to devote all of their energies and skills to their professions. Also required is a commitment—an internal gyroscope that points an ultimate direction from which there can be no permanent deviation.

The young man interested in a political career will then ask: "Beyond education, what?" The answer at this point is obvious. Local community participation, of course, is extremely important to initial ventures into politics. The average citizen can do much to improve some aspect of his community's life. Inevitably this brings him into contact with community politics. If he wants to run for office eventually, he naturally must become directly engaged in political affairs. The task requires time and effort, humor and patience. It means joining a party, a clubhouse, and a candidate. Soon the aspirant will discover that he is involved, and he may be involved for good.

The second question is asked of me and, I am sure, of every practicing politician by thoughtful spectators: "What of the need for compromise? Is there room for morality in politics?" The question is always a good one and is equally applicable to international and domestic politics; in this context, not much difference exists between the two.

One can find various answers. A favorite of mine is that of Justice Oliver Wendell Holmes, "I do accept a rough equation between isness and oughtness." There is also the expression of a careful member of Congress when he casts a vote he does not really believe in but votes in the interests of a longer range strategy, or simply as a matter of party regularity: "Well, occasionally I find it necessary to rise above principle."

Throughout history political leaders have wrestled with the question of compromise. Among those who struggled most deeply in our past was Woodrow Wilson. A genuine Christian moralist, Wilson had this to say in 1917: "As always, the right will prove to be the expedient."

Nations, said Wilson on another occasion, must be bound in their conduct and in their relations with each other "by the same principles of honor and of respect for the common law of civilized societies that govern the individual citizens of all modern states in their relations with one another . . ."

These propositions—that there is an ultimate harmony between moral principles and human self-interest and that a nation is a servant bound by those principles and is not an end in itself—have been debated by men in public life since the beginning of civilization. The discourse is not yet resolved.

Those who contend that the affairs of state are a realm immune from the requirements of conscience often describe themselves as "realists," which implies that ideals are somehow not "real" and that those in public life who believe in the pursuit of ideals are intrinsically incapable of realism. I believe a plea should be made for the reality of ideals.

The self-designated "realists" in public life base their approach to public policy on the assumption that the essence of politics is a permanent and relentless struggle for power in which we have no choice but to accept a tragic, irremediable moral discrepancy between means and ends. Rivalry and strife, they tell us, are the rule of politics and not a mere accident. To act wisely, say the "realists," we must accept this premise and formulate our policies within its confines.

The "realist" philosophy is set forth thoroughly and skill-fully by Professor Hans Morgenthau of the University of Chicago. In his book *Politics Among Nations,* Professor Morgenthau advises us to adjust our policies to the proposition that only "shreds and fragments" of an old universal morality survive in the modern world, that we have returned to the "politics and morality of tribalism, of the Crusades, and of the religious wars." So eminent a diplomatist and his-torian as George F. Kennan contends that a legalist-moralist approach has been the most serious defect of American for-eign policy over the past half-century.

At the opposite pole from the "realist" are those detached visionaries or "utopians" who view the struggle for power as an abnormal and passing phase of our political life, dis-missing evil from the affairs of man by fiat—not because it is absent, but because they *wish* it were. The "utopian" sees a millennium of human virtue and happiness around every historical corner, to be realized by the simplest of reforms, by the cleansing at a stroke of our political souls.

We can best judge ourselves by our historical perform-ance, and it is a melancholy fact that human history lends no more credence to the tenets of the "utopians" than to those of the "realists."

A third position, more subtle and complex, is more closely aligned, I think, to the reality of public life as we have known it. This approach—one of "practical idealism"—

takes full cognizance of the reality of ambition, greed, and ruthlessness in man's comportment, but gives due regard to his demonstrated aspiration toward moral and spiritual fulfillment. Such a view of human nature, when applied to politics, suggests the validity of what Professor Arnold Wolfers defines as a *"non-perfectionist ethic,"* a set of moral goals and values which we must attempt to realize in our political life while recognizing that our attempts are often likely to fail. Moreover, the "practical idealist" in public life accepts the necessity of compromise, concession, adjustment, and strategic retreat in the pursuit of a morally worthy objective. And in extreme conditions—surely when the survival of the nation itself is at stake—the *"practical idealist"* statesman will not shrink from using the methods and policies of power politics.

Occasionally it is necessary to stand firmly and uncompromisingly on a principle that is bound up in an issue of the time; even when it is foreordained to defeat. Those are moments or days that may come infrequently to the practitioner, but any one of them might be worth his whole tour of office. He may be stamped a loser as a result. But it may also give meaning to his entire adventure into politics.

11

The Republican Party, History and Tradition

THE PHILOSOPHY of the Republican Party evolved from a log cabin in a simple and lovely American town. It drew strength from the ruggedness of green, uncut country. It came to the crowded cities and awakened and inspired the new millions. In Abraham Lincoln, the patron of that philosophy, millions found the pride of personal service. Lincoln radiated strength with forbearance. He lifted each man out of the heap and gave him a sense of belonging to something bigger than his immediate station. Lincoln's was an uncomplicated theme. It was understood and it had appeal. Possibly it meant different things to different people, but to all, ultimately, it promised greater individual self-respect, dignity, and freedom.

To Lincoln, people were the only proper repositories of

power. People sensed this in him. To many, his outlook defined their concept of freedom. They understood that Lincoln would give leadership, and he did—unshakable, powerful leadership—but they felt in him also a pervading sense that power cannot be used by any political leader in our democratic society as a feudal image.

"If there is anything which it is the duty of the whole people never to entrust to any hands but their own," said Lincoln, "that is the preservation and perpetuity of their own liberties and institutions."

The Republican Party must take on the special task of defining the role of the individual in the midst of our part garrison, part welfare state. It must establish guideposts for unfettered individual betterment, and open avenues for the pursuit of individual excellence. It must spell out in understandable terms that the real danger of modern central government is the pervasive threat to individual liberties that stems from any undue concentration of power.

Those liberties include the right to speak freely and critically, to associate with anyone or any group, to travel, to take up unpopular causes, to be unafraid of "the possible tyranny of the majority" and to avoid the frustration and pettiness of weighty bureaucracy. The Republican Party must demonstrate that a concentration of power through a government-dominated industrial-military complex may be just as threatening to steady economic growth and to individual freedoms as are all other excessive power groupings. It must argue that the proper role of government in our country is to create the framework under and around which free, nongovernment economic, social, and cultural institutions may flourish. The Republican Party must understand also that safeguarding of individual worth includes the creation or protection of basic conditions of living that will not permit any person, who cannot help himself, to live below a minimum standard of decency in a civilized nation. We have done a great deal in this country for organizations and power groups; it is time we thought more about individuals who increasingly have become subordinate to organizations or helpless among power groups.

And, finally, Republicans must attune themselves to world affairs with a far greater awareness and maturity than any party or President has been able to do in this century.

Both the major political parties are often demonstrated to be a collection of factions and warring groups, a strange coalition of opposites. The Democratic Party has at one and the same time happily embraced anti-civil rights interests and illiberal doctrines in some areas and liberal courses in other areas. In the big cities of the North it has shaped itself into machine governments which have been as inward-grown and regressive as their allies of convenience in the South. Often it is only the perpetuation of a status quo—most often patronage—which has been the motivational force. Power has been used or taken either for the feeding process or for its own sake.

The Republican Party by the same token has embraced warring notions concerning what government is all about to such an extent as to immobilize the party. Its liberal and conservative divisions—found in almost every community—

have held each other almost to a stand-off, except in 1964 when the rightists shoved the centrists out altogether. The result has been a clinging to the status quo, which has meant remaining out of power even in those areas where the Democratic alternative has seemed for the average intelligent voter almost equally unattractive.

The Republican Party should adjust the framework of the government, central and local, according to individual needs and strict priorities of importance within the bounds of power and money which the people are willing to give to government. It should offer government that tolerates dissent and individuality, that serves rather than dominates, and that has a mature sense of responsibility and of America's greatness in world affairs. It should mobilize the private sector towards a new commitment to the cities of the nation.

It can be argued that this could be anybody's platform. And yet it is the hardest to follow. It requires selectivity in the use of power, priorities in program, and imagination in dealing with local interests at home or abroad.

This is the future of the Republican Party. It is a bright future but it will come to pass only if Republicans move with a changing country and a changing world, and remember the lessons of history.

The history of the great leaders of the Republican Party has been an enlightened one. It can be described as a history of wisdom and effectiveness in power, responsibility in opposition. Men cast in this mold, whether in power or in opposition, have always been distinguished by fidelity to our heritage, a vibrant awareness of public needs and public interests, and a strong sense of the movement of history. Such men, when entrusted with office, have exercised power with wisdom and effectiveness; while in opposition they have fulfilled their twofold obligation of constructive criticism and responsibility to the nation.

The tradition calls for courage. It may and often is accomplished with searing adversity. Lincoln heard few tributes in his lifetime. He was always running uphill, forever standing up against a barrage of kicks, not a few of them delivered by members of his own party. When Lincoln came up for a second term in office after three years of the "grinding drama of drums, blood, and agony," hardly a member of Congress dared speak out to advocate a second term for the President. Carl Sandburg points out that in early 1864 only one Congressman in the House of Representatives was definitely committed to Lincoln, and he was from Illinois. "The opposition to Mr. Lincoln," wrote Indiana Republican Congressman George W. Julian, "was secretly cherished by many of the ablest and most patriotic men of the day. . . . Of the more earnest and thorough-going Republicans in both Houses of Congress probably not one in ten really favored his renomination." A "Committee of Prominent Senators and Representatives" issued a "Confidential" circular bitterly attacking Lincoln and urging the nomination of Chase. As so often happens with "secret" documents in politics, the full text was reprinted in the newspapers. "Go on, Gentlemen! Wash your dirty linen in public," jibed the Democratic *New York World*.

Lincoln was renominated and went on to fight a blistering

campaign. On election night the re-elected President spoke from the White House by torchlight: "It has long been a grave question," Lincoln said, "whether any government, not too strong for the liberties of its people, can be strong enough to maintain its own existence in great emergencies." In a single sentence he summed up an aspect of his Republican credo that has, ever since, been a chief concern of the Republican Party. It has been a concern with balance; a recognition that the totalitarian abuse of power is not always far from its essential utilitarian use. Lincoln refused to reach out for popularity at a time when it might have been his. Although he was an enormously skillful politician, the modern-day concepts of "image," charisma, or "mystique" mattered little to him.

President Rutherford B. Hayes faced head on one of the most controversial subjects of his time—the spoils system, and introduced Civil Service as the means of governmental employment and tenure. It is thought that this more than anything led to his failure to win nomination for a second term. His contribution, and political sacrifice, was lasting.

Our country and the Republican Party have been strengthened by the Taft family. The first of their notable public servants, William Howard Taft, deserved greater tribute than he received during or after his lifetime. He was savagely attacked during his tenure of office because of his rigorously constitutional view of the powers of the Presidency.

After leaving public office, he became the unofficial leader of the citizens' movement for a league of nations. He worked tirelessly for a world body with enforcement powers. He gave wise counsel and faithful support to President Wilson. He made a distinguished effort that was little appreciated. He received no reward, except perhaps the personal satisfaction that he was responsible in opposition.

Taft was never quite Republican enough to please his Republican colleagues. Speaker of the House Joe Cannon said of him, "the trouble with Taft is that if he were Pope he would find it necessary to appoint a few Protestant Cardinals."

Said Taft, "I have tried to do in each case what seemed to me the wisest thing, regardless of its effect upon my own future. Indeed, in more than one case I have been perfectly conscious bad blood would be stirred by some act of mine or some refusal to act. The circumstances that the same persons who hail me, after one application of equal justice, as a far-seeing, conservative patriot, denounce me after the next as an unreasoning radical, does not greatly disturb my equanimity."

Taft spoke for many a man or woman in public life. Who in elective office has not felt the barbs of public reproach from those who think of "liberal" versus "conservative" attitudes as so many pigeonholes, each carefully labeled black or white, god or devil?

Effectiveness in power and responsibility in opposition was also the motivating principle of his son Robert A. Taft, who was a liberal in the best sense of the word. He cared about the individual and his future, and he gave of himself totally, for his country, and for his party. I am gratified that there is in the same tradition another Taft, Robert Jr., with whom I had the privilege of serving in the House of Representatives.

My own state of New York has given men like Theodore Roosevelt, Henry Stimson, Elihu Root, Charles Evans Hughes, and Thomas Dewey. These were men whose credos as "progressive conservatives," to use Stimson's own description, were built on their conviction, first, that the primary and overriding requirement of all government is that it should not infringe upon the essential liberties of the individual, and, second, that within this limitation government could and must be made a powerful instrument for the enhancement of individual citizens by group action. Nelson Rockefeller, the present Governor of New York, follows in this tradition. So do the Republican Senators of the post-World War II period: Ives, Javits, and Keating.

In 1931 Henry Stimson, as Herbert Hoover's Secretary of State, in the face of an isolationist public opinion, enunciated the "Stimson Doctrine"—that the United States would not recognize the fruits of aggression. Under this Doctrine a moral embargo was imposed against Japan by the United States in the wake of the Japanese assault on the peace of 1919 by its aggression in Manchuria in 1931. The "Stimson Doctrine" was the first post-World War I expression of conscience of the United States in international affairs, coupled with positive action which was as firm as the circumstances of the time allowed.

Stimson fought hard for the re-election of Herbert Hoover thereafter. Upon defeat he, like Hoover, helped ease the transition of the successor government and withdrew to retirement. Many years later, when World War II was going badly for the Allies, Stimson was called back into government service by a Democratic President. He ran the War Department with energy, dedication, and decisiveness, culminating his career with the awesome task of guiding a new and unprepared President in the climactic final days of the war. It was Stimson who briefed President Truman on the existence of the "Manhattan Project," the atom bomb, and it was Stimson who served as the President's most intimate advisor in the agonizing process which led to the decision to use the new weapon against Japan.

Wendell Willkie and Thomas E. Dewey recharged the Republican Party with a sense of modernism and international responsibility. They laid the foundations upon which such men as Arthur Vandenberg could build even more. "A political party," declared Willkie, "could never stand still. . . . Those leaders of a party who insist on applying old formulas to present problems merely because those formulas worked in the past are damaging the party and will eventually destroy it. For these are standing still, whereas the world around them moves."

Arthur Vandenberg achieved a place in history by his role as a statesman who helped forge a foreign policy for the West at a time when half the world was on its knees. The Marshall Plan probably would have been impossible without Vandenberg's powerful advocacy in a Republican Congress. As a delegate to the San Francisco Conference, it was Vandenberg who was responsible for some of the most con-

structive and farsighted provisions of the United Nations
Charter. He successfully fought down the Soviet effort to
hobble the General Assembly with restrictions on the scope
of its deliberations. It was at Vandenberg's tenacious insistence that the Soviets yielded on their demand for a total
veto in the Security Council, embracing procedural as well
as substantive questions. He also was largely responsible for
Article 51 of the Charter which is the legal basis of NATO,
indeed of our entire collective security system. Here was extraordinary foresight, for it was the famous "Vandenberg
Resolution" of 1948 which gave President Truman the man-
date of a Republican Congress for the negotiation of the
North Atlantic Treaty. Vandenberg, as loyal a Republican
as one can find in the history of our Party, must have known
that Harry Truman would claim partisan credit for accom-
plishment which he, Vandenberg, had made possible. It was
perhaps an unpleasant price to pay for the rewards of responsible opposition, but Vandenberg paid it, knowing that
the stakes of history far exceeded personal vanities and partisan interests.

Eisenhower attained renown as a statesman-general under
Democratic Presidents. It fell to him to heal the ugly schisms
that had developed within the country's body politic during
the closing years of a long Democratic era. Through the
years of his administration he brought a needed unity to the
nation. Although he was later criticized for not exercising
the fullest possible control over his own party, his concept
of a United States with pre-eminence in foreign affairs—a
status achieved apart from domestic politics—lent a sureness

and stability to a world more unstable and perilous than people then realized.

During the later Eisenhower years few realized the extent of the right-wing movement within the Republican Party. It was more of a negative than a positive force—a resentment against the "Eastern Establishment" and against Federal entry of any kind except as directed against Communism wherever it might be found, and whatever its gradation.

Anti-Federalism finally centered on the Civil Rights Act of 1964. Despite its Republican initiatives and its consistency with Republican platforms over the years, it was this issue that brought to a head the growing Republican division in the Goldwater year.

The day the deadlock was broken and the Civil Rights Act of 1964 was reported out of the Judiciary Committee ready for action by the whole House of Representatives, a furled umbrella was placed surreptitiously on Charlie Halleck's desk on the floor of the House, in plain view of the galleries. Charles Halleck was the Republican Minority Leader. He had just agreed to give Republican leadership support to this compromise, but still sweeping, national approach to Civil Rights, thereby backing the long efforts of the Republican progressives to force the issue within both the Congress and the Administration. But the New Right within the Republican Party had a different view of what the party should stand for. Thus the umbrella, symbol of appeasement and weakness, was delivered to the traditionalist Old Guard by the militant New Right—the first public eruption on Capitol Hill of the colliding pressures that had been building below and that five months later at the Cow Palace convention were to split the soul of the G.O.P.

It did not take long for power to change hands after the groundwork was done. Five months after the Civil Rights Act had passed the House of Representatives and the delegates had taken over, the Republican "Moderates," as they became known, were defeated at the Cow Palace Convention in a two-to-one vote against strengthening the Civil Rights plank of the platform. There were two other roll call votes at the convention, one on the issue of "extremism" and the other on the question of military commanders' discretionary powers to use tactical nuclear weapons. The atmosphere was not conducive to rational debate (Governor Rockefeller was booed mercilessly as he tried to speak from the rostrum) and the moderates went down each time to a howling defeat. I recall musing to a fellow delegate that a pro-motherhood resolution would have been howled down by that crowd on that particular evening. Later, about two in the morning, when the battle of the platform was over and the convention hall lay in a pile of litter, a minister was giving the benediction, calling upon God for guidance. A delegate, whom I did not know, standing near me with bowed head, nudged me with his elbow and muttered, "Vote, 'No.'"

Thus ended phase one of the battle for the heart of the G.O.P. Its power structure was now oriented West and South. It was hostile to the East and deeply suspicious of the egalitarianism of the cities. It had been a centrist party which for decades had occupied the middle ground between

Right and Left. Now it had veered Right, but its offerings for the sixties and seventies were yet to be defined or fully discovered.

The campaign and election proved that the strange brand of "conservatism" which manifested itself was a total negativism that offered little toward the solution of the complex problems of the last third of the twentieth century. Although aspects of the campaign undoubtedly were consistent with traditional Republican economic conservatism, it was lost upon the country. The campaign exhibited a puzzling unreality, a mysticism that gripped the insiders but frightened the outsiders. It seemed suicidal—a kind of political kamikaze against which there was no defense by reason.

The avalanche that took place on election day swept out legions of Republican officeholders across the land. Over six hundred Republican state and city legislators lost their seats. Thirty-eight Republican Congressmen went down to defeat, among them the strongest Goldwater supporters and others who had opposed his nomination but chose to support him later. In these categories were seven Republican Congressmen from New York State, mainly from traditionally Republican upstate districts, and the one remaining Republican Congressman from Connecticut. The latter, Abner Sibal, progressive and effective, had strongly opposed Goldwater at San Francisco but had given him a nominal endorsement later. The right-wing elements abandoned him in the election for insufficient support while independents voted against him in droves for having endorsed at all.

My own decision shortly after the Cow Palace convention was to declare independence from the national ticket. It was a difficult decision because it meant a major party break and, apart from the strains of a complicated election battle that year (the Conservative Party ran a pro-Goldwater candidate in the 17th District), it would not be forgotten.

I recall most clearly writing my three-page statement of independence from the national ticket. I retired to my apartment on West Fifty-eighth Street at eight o'clock in the evening on a Friday with several pads of yellow legal-size paper, a couple of martinis, a quart of milk, a jar of peanut butter, jam, and a loaf of bread. I quit at three o'clock in the morning with yellow paper scattered all over the floor and a finished draft ready to be reread and restudied in the morning and over the weekend.

On Tuesday morning, August 4, I made public my statement, which follows in slightly condensed form:

The principles for which I have worked in Congress are being challenged in this election by the Conservative Party. The Party, made up chiefly of key supporters of Senator Goldwater, is running its former New York State Chairman against me in the 17th Congressional District.

Instead of the party unity that is preached by the most ardent supporters of Senator Goldwater in New York, my re-election to Congress as the regular Republican candidate is now opposed by these same forces. The Conservative party, as our Republican state chairman, Fred A. Young, has stated, is "an opposition party publicly committed to campaign for the defeat and destruction of the Republican Party in New York."

The Conservative Party and its early organizers for Senator Goldwater in New York State are bent on a course of destruction in the 17th Congressional District. I have no choice but to fight back with all of the strength at my command.*

I will fight with equal strength against the attacks being made on me and my record from the opposite direction by the nominee of the Democratic and Liberal parties.

At the San Francisco convention earlier this year, I fought for the principles I believe are embedded in the Republican Party's history and tradition and from which I have no intention of retreating.

Along with other Republicans from all parts of the country, I carried the fight to the Platform Committee of which I was a member, and finally to the rostrum of the full convention. In the months before the convention I argued the case for these principles in a dozen states, from Massachusetts to Oregon.

The convention refused to reassert traditional Republican beliefs in such matters as civilian control over the military in the use of nuclear weapons; in the rule of law over rule by whatever extremist group might prevail; and in our commitment to the rightness of and necessity for a body of national law under which each man may enjoy life, liberty, and the pursuit of happiness according to his merits rather than according to his race, his religion, or his national origin.

These are foremost among the long-established tenets of the Republican Party; yet the convention of 1964 would not acknowledge them even when their merit had been put directly in issue.

To those allied to basic Republican principles, principles

* It should be noted that the Conservative Party fielded candidates against the Republican Party nominees in New York State in the two subsequent years, as well. They opposed me in the 1965 New York City Mayoralty election and Governor Rockefeller in his 1966 re-election campaign.

which have been disavowed by the uncompromising proponents of a Conservative Party candidate who is running against me in the general election, it should be clear that I have no choice but to run in this election on my own record, without reference to the national ticket.

To do otherwise, as long as these circumstances exist, would be to retreat from principle and to assist the Conservative Party and its organizers who in New York seek to defeat me and the party principles for which traditional Republicans always have stood.

I intend to campaign for and with Republican state and local candidates who have kept faith with the century-old heritage of the Republican Party. And I intend to work with like-minded Republicans throughout the United States.

Republicans across the country who believe in the party of Lincoln should join hands and work together for the rededication of the Republican Party to those principles which have made the party in the past the center core of America.

I have found that much touted differences between geographical areas are far less than is commonly thought, and most certainly far less than would appear from the San Francisco convention. And I have found that there are many thousands of Republicans all over the United States who feel as I do and who will also work within the party for their beliefs. I intend to work tirelessly with them, as I have in the past.

I believe in the great history and tradition of the Republican Party which in the past has had the wisdom never to be scornful of the old, nor afraid of the new. I am resolved to defend that history and tradition from those who would destroy it. I hope that the people of the 17th Congressional District, who for six years I have had the honor to represent in Congress, will support me in that effort.

They did. When the ballots were tabulated, I had received 135,807 votes to 44,533 votes for the Democratic-Liberal candidate. The candidate of the Conservative Party received 9,491 votes. The 91,000-vote plurality was reported to be the largest given any opposed Republican candidate for Congress in the 1964 general elections. When the votes were counted, I was very proud to be a Republican.

The odd part about 1964 was that the great majority of Republican Governors across the country, and many of the Republican Senators, who also ran state-wide, were and are progressives. Each had dealt realistically with the problems of his state. They followed a solid tradition. Republican Presidents over the last century who represented the moderate theme were men who recognized that policy essentially is a response to demonstrated needs and demands.

I trust this will be true again. When populations, like ours, are growing and on the move, and whole continents are swept up in drives of nationalism and unrest, a party philosophy is no philosophy which merely rests on the assumption that there is no government responsibility whatever.

The powers of government must always be checked and balanced, and this remains a Republican credo, but even this principle must be related to national and international growth. In their hundred-year history Republicans in power have been best at finding that balance between public and private uses that guards against mediocrity (always the danger of a too greatly planned society), that reaches for excellence by respecting individual responsibility, that resists blind conformity, but which at the same time understands the use of government—namely, to create a social order in which every human being can live in dignity, respect law, and receive justice, and exploit endlessly the best in himself.

As this volume goes to press, the election results of 1966 are completed and Republicans identified as moderate progressives throughout most of the country were elected. Republican moderates and progressives in the Congress for the most part increased their majorities.

Winners in 1966, Edward Brooke and Elliott Richardson of Massachusetts, John Chafee of Rhode Island, Robert Griffin of Michigan, Mark Hatfield of Oregon, Charles Percy of Illinois, the Rockefellers—in New York and Arkansas —and George Romney of Michigan prove the durability of the Republican Party and the two-party system as we have become accustomed to it.

Republican moderates and centrists of the past and present have offered unrevolutionary and, happily, unsystematic change in both domestic and world affairs. Their accomplishments should be remembered and their advice heeded. More than forty years ago, former President Theodore Roosevelt warned the Republicans in Congress that the world was changing. He said: "Mere negation and obstruction and attempts to revive the dead past spell ruin." He was right then and his words, I believe, are just as right now.

12

Commitment to the City

On MAY 13, 1965, I announced I would run for Mayor of New York City. The decision had been reached only about a week earlier, and marked the resolution of a dilemma that my wife and I had been thrashing out for several months. At one point, early in March, I had decided against becoming involved in the Mayoralty, but I'm not certain that at any point I was entirely comfortable with the decision; the question kept returning.

Family considerations seemed to oppose my running. Mary, the children (including now our son John, born in 1959), and I had become accustomed to, and liked, the life of a Congressman. We were living in Washington, having shifted our home and the children's schooling from New

York three years earlier. During my first four years in Congress, we had kept our home in New York. But with a ten-month Congress being the rule rather than the exception, any kind of a home life for a full-time Congressman was impossible unless his family was in Washington. We felt we had just barely settled ourselves and we were happy in our new home.

Mary and I both knew, however, that we were in political life neither for comfort nor permanence. One day, not too distant, we would have to make some basic personal decisions. Perhaps this was the time. New York City was in trouble. There was much talk about the crisis in the cities, New York particularly, but few did anything about it. It seemed tragic that the responsibility for running a city should, year after year, be avoided rather than sought.

My earlier decision not to run was based largely upon a knowledge of the hard logistics of running. Winning appeared all but impossible; an overwhelming defeat was more likely. Many of those who urged running would not be around when the tough chores needed doing—raising enormous amounts of money, organizing blocks in the five boroughs, rounding up the elusive facts and figures with which the issues would be fought out. Even assuming a million and a half dollars could be raised, the campaign would require a personal commitment of six months of full-time, seven-day-week running. My Congressional duties would have to be cut back. I would have to neglect my children, live with exhaustion, and mollify the continual complainers.

If by some chance I won, I would have to do things that

would outrage the very people who initially supported my candidacy. I knew how much trouble the City was in, and how much worse it could get before the tide of deterioration was stemmed.

Among those who pressed the hardest for my running were John H. Whitney and Walter Thayer of the *New York Herald Tribune*. They were consistent in their support and met their pledges to aid in the financing. My long-time advisers, Herbert Brownell and Charles Metzner, were doubtful about the wisdom of running. They were even more dubious about the probability of halting the decline of the city, or, in the process, coping with its political power structure. But they supported my decision. As before, my brothers, and my law partners, Beth Webster and Fred Sheffield, were with me no matter what I might decide. Ultimately, Bob Price agreed. For Bob, the decision was most difficult, for he would have to manage an uphill, city-wide campaign. He did—brilliantly and successfully.

The final decision on my part was made, as I have said, about a week before I announced. Mary, the three older children, and I gathered in the small library of our home and I consulted with the children. They were unusually adult in their opinions and in their questions. They knew it was a terribly important decision, for them as well as for their parents. I believe they even sensed it would result in some disruptions they would not like, but they supported my proposal that I enter the race—even more strongly than I would have thought.

A factor in my decision was the change in the attitude of

people about cities, a change that was becoming noticeable. It was a change that had to come. For our country has been undergoing a most complicated urban revolution, comparable in scope to the industrial revolution of the last century; the pressures within it are just as complex and as explosive as were the pressures of that earlier age. Whether we can survive these explosive pressures, whether we can guide them into productive channels leading to a happier and more humane environment in the cities, is one of the most severe tests of our civilization.

Personal involvement alone cannot meet the test. Public institutions, most especially municipal government itself, must change. Fortunately, this imperative frequently is self-enforcing; all across the nation, the ills of urban living are prompting a growing demand for sweeping changes in big-city government. The alarming truth is that the cities of the United States must find the strength to govern themselves far better, or poverty will erode them, crime will continue to prosper, their economies will wither, and our faith in the ability of the democratic process to govern an urban society will diminish.

The nation must make an extraordinary new investment in its sagging, often debilitated cities. This will require Federal talent as well as Federal billions. But no army of technicians, no amount of Federal billions, can fill the void left by an absence of a soundly structured city government.

New York stands out as an American city that is the biggest, the tallest, the most crowded, the most hurried; the noisiest, liveliest, freshest, and toughest. But because it is the biggest, it is also the most problem-filled city of all. The ills of urban life and the failure of city government have been more evident in New York than elsewhere because of its sheer size, just as its bright lights stand out with greater clarity than those of any other city.

It seems to me that the successful—or, more humbly, the efficient—operation of a big city begins with the "urbanists." An "urbanist" is a modern man who is probably more finely trained in the complicated business of present and future domestic government than any other public servant in history. He usually has a deep knowledge of the workings of the Federal government, both in the executive and the legislative branches. He understands state government. And above all, he must know the vast reaches and depths and infinite complexities of the big city.

Traditional political power structures in big cities have little understanding of the urbanist. The urbanist brings in a whole new world, a world of Washington, of large and complicated programs, of science, design, and planning. It is a world almost wholly foreign to the precinct power dealer.

Leadership is a critical issue in the cities, but we never can recruit enough trained professionals and urbanists for executive positions in the cities if we rule out large numbers of them because they happen to belong to the "wrong" political party. That, perhaps, may help to explain why so many of our cities are in desperate trouble; they have tried to combat the crush of urban problems with one arm in a partisan sling.

The traditional politician in a big city can bring one im-

portant segment of information to government operations:
What people are against, and why. Rarely can he interpret
what people are for, except in such vague terms as "for
housing," "for better schools," "for equal rights." Clear,
specific solutions are not the forte of the political leaders of
today's large cities.

All of which has led many cities to the conclusion that
the ordinary concept of Republicans and Democrats as opposing forces in city affairs is obsolete. From Boston to
Los Angeles, from Atlanta to Seattle, almost 100 major
American cities have chosen nonpartisan Mayors. Many
of those cities, like New York, are at the core of great
metropolitan areas.

One has only to attend a conference of the Nation's
Mayors to discover the similarity of their problems and the
immediacy of their needs and frustrations. They can't afford the luxury of dialectic about Republicans and Democrats. They have neither the time nor the money for
partisan skirmishes; not with an entire sea of civic controversy pressing in on them. They already labor from
morning until night with non-political problems; purely
partisan disputes intrude upon time and patience. After
all, as Fiorello LaGuardia once observed, there is no Republican way to pave a street and no Democratic way to
lay a sewer, no Republican formula for making traffic jams
disappear and no infallible Democratic prescription for
preventing crime.

Republicans and Democrats properly express positions
on budgetary allocations by the Federal Government, on

the scope of the country's foreign aid programs, and on the nation's agricultural policies. It is their function to do so. Local parties and governments, however, are more directly involved with people than with ideologies. City government is where the public agency, the public servant, and the public come together. City government concerns where and how Americans live, and the condition of most cities today should leave little room for partisan divisions as we strive to make the streets safe, the housing livable, and the schools conducive to the learning process. The very complexity of modern urban life argues most eloquently for the abandonment of traditional partisanship in municipal government, for that complexity transcends any ward or precinct.

New York itself contains thousands of neighborhood associations, dozens of nationalities, ethnic strains from all the globe—a pluralistic society of such diversity that no one political party can remotely claim to represent it adequately.

The need to reorganize local government along bipartisan lines is nowhere greater than in New York, if for no other reason than its administrative hugeness. New York City's budget is exceeded in the United States only by that of the Federal Government. Its population is larger than 67 of 117 members of the United Nations. Its police force of more than twenty-eight thousand men is larger than many national armies. New York City is the equivalent of more than two Chicagos or four Philadelphias. If each of the five boroughs that compose New York were a separate city, they would comprise four of the eight largest cities in the country.

For all these reasons, I pledged to re-establish in New York City a nonpartisan government—a fusion of diverse political interests for the single purpose of achieving good government.

Fusion government had been adopted four times previously in New York City, and it succeeded, in the main, every time. The people elected a fusion Mayor in 1894, and the city's streets were clean for the first time in twenty years. They elected a fusion Mayor in 1901, and obtained new schools, improved public-health and water-supply operations, tenement-house law enforcement, and honest government. They elected a fusion Mayor in 1913 and obtained their first city zoning, a modernized administration, sound finances, a model health department, and high-caliber men in public offices.

In 1933 the people of New York City elected Fiorello LaGuardia. The following twelve years of fusion government brought the most refreshing era of change and reform New York had ever known. Mayor LaGuardia restored the city's credit. He reformed the Civil Service. He was the scourge of big-time racketeers and vice-lords. He pioneered public housing in New York City. He instituted municipal health insurance. He revamped city government with a new charter.

Thus history argues compellingly for the value of fusion government, which, in bringing new leadership combinations to power, brought needed changes to the people.

In New York during the post-war years, change was associated chiefly with decline: As the city's problems intensified, they became symbolic of all of an urban society's shortcomings, and New York was more and more characterized as ungovernable. Critics pointed to the ensnarled traffic, the crumbling tenements, the littered streets, the fouled air and water, and concluded that the city had become unmanageable.

These conditions remain visible and real; they are the manifestations of an ailing city, one which needs hard work, imagination, and money if it is to meet the many problems of an urban age.

Although these difficulties cannot be belittled, it became clear to me as a candidate that a primary source of New York's troubles was the structure of city government itself. It had grown, like the urban sprawl around it, into an unplanned hodgepodge of fragmented agencies, departments and bureaus, too inflexible or undirected to deal with the city's problems effectively.

I believed as a candidate, and believe now, that New York City can be governed economically and efficiently. I base that belief upon the enactment of a sensible realignment of the city's administrative machinery—a project I began to carry out soon after taking office.

The reorganization's principal function is to bring under one roof functions and responsibilities now assigned somewhat irrationally and expensively to several branches of city government; specifically, to establish ten administrations incorporating the functions of almost fifty separate departments and agencies. They would be named: Corrections; Economic Development; Environmental Protection; Financial Management; General Services; Health Services; Housing and Development; Human Resources; Recreation and Cultural Affairs; Transportation. The Police, Fire and Investigations Departments would continue as separate entities, directly responsible to the Mayor.

The regrouping is designed to expedite and strengthen both the programming of city services and the actual delivery of those services. Reorganization will facilitate the planning of major programs to anticipate and deal with various problems before they become flaming crises. One of the reasons that the city often appears to be in a perpetual state of siege is that the flow of relevant information necessary to anticipate such crises must push its way through the bureaucracy's maddening maze of dams and baffles.

Agencies of the city continuously grapple with fractions of problems transcending their own jurisdictions. The ensuing divisiveness requires city departments to deal with each other almost by treaty. The process inevitably obfuscates and frequently compromises eventual solutions, for department and agency heads often are obliged, like the blind men in the fable, to guess the nature of the elephant from the small handholds they are able to grasp. It is not surprising that they often guess wrong. The continuance of the system probably was best explained by a Federal official who spent his lifetime in the highest levels of government service: "The nearest approach to immortality on earth," he reflected, "is a government bureau."

The consolidation of almost fifty of New York's departments and agencies into ten administrations clearly will
have the effect of centralizing city government. But we are
correspondingly interested in the decentralization of government. The two objectives are not inconsistent, for I draw
a distinction between centralization of the decision-making
process and decentralization of the process by which the
results of those decisions are delivered to the neighborhoods.
It is entirely possible to create a single department to decide which streets are to be repaved while giving the people in our various communities a fuller voice in designating
which streets have the highest priority.

Indeed, my conviction is that the city must create new
relationships between government and the community—
relationships by which the disbursement of city services
may be coordinated at the community level and guided by
community need. These relationships should complement
locally the reorganization that is needed centrally.

More sensible and constructive relationships must be
achieved, also, between the central cities of America and
the communities surrounding them. "Surrounding" may be
too flat a word; some mayors would replace it with "drain-
ing" or "choking." My own view is that envy, selfishness
and hostility in our metropolitan areas vitiated the creation
of a better liaison between the core city and its satellites.
The swift conversion of this country to an urban society
demands that the metropolitan units of government join together to bring order and reason to that transformation.

The New York metropolitan area, for example, embraces portions of three states, twenty-two counties, and fourteen hundred local governments. A variety of interstate organizations and the state and Federal governments are inter-mixed with the affairs of all these entities. This is urban sprawl, as well as urban crisis, and it cannot be dealt with effectively within the narrow confines of traditional partisanship—if for no other reason than that political chicanery will paralyze any effort to reach broad resolutions of public policy.

Nor can it be dealt with effectively if Americans continue to believe that they can both escape the travails of the city by moving to the suburbs and continue to enjoy the myriad benefits of the city they left behind. They cannot attain the best of both worlds, for if the central city disintegrates, it does not do so in a vacuum; its fall will mean the sure decline of the surrounding communities. There can be no Larchmont without New York City; no Sausalito without San Francisco; no Winnetka without Chicago and no Webster Groves without St. Louis.

The central city provides suburbanites with their jobs, their theatre, their sports, their museums and art galleries, their transportation terminals, their restaurants, their brokers, and physicians, their identity as metropolitan citizens.

The suburban communities must realize that their strength—in fine homes, outstanding schools, convenient shopping centers—is directly contingent upon the strength of the core city. Conversely, the ills of the core city are not readily confined to municipal boundaries, and most of our suburbs are learning that lesson. In the affluent suburbs of New York City, the costs of welfare are soaring. Juvenile delinquency is increasing more rapidly than in the cities. Industry is moving in, often despite the loud protests of homeowners in the vicinity. And taxes are going up and up, chiefly to accommodate burgeoning enrollments in the public school systems.

It is, then, neither rational nor practicable to place the central city and its suburbs in separate, isolated categories. We have common problems and we must seek mutual solutions. Basic to any metropolitan solution, however, is the renascence of the city that serves as the nucleus of the metropolis, a reconstruction in which the Federal government should be the major architect.

In New York City, we seek a more creative relationship with the Federal government, which is our chief hope for financial assistance, and that is why I have placed so much emphasis on equipping city government with professional officials and a modern, compact chain of command.

Only within the last ten years has Washington begun to channel its power and resources into the problems of the cities, and even then, Congress usually has moved with misgivings or restraint. One reason is the pervasive suspicion that Federal funds spent in the cities are likely to be dissipated or diverted; in short, that Federal allocations will be wasted because the cities themselves are incapable of honest, conscientious, progressive administration.

As a former Congressman, I know the suspicion exists. As a Mayor, I am trying to prove it wrong in New York

City. For I think we are facing up to the realities of governing our cities, and one is that we must put our own house in order to obtain the state and Federal assistance we demonstrably need if cities are to continue as the summation of this country's culture and civilization.

Historically, it should be noted, no civilization has ever flourished in the absence of strong, dynamic cities.

A second reality, in my judgment, is that the Federal Government, with its enormously productive taxing powers, must pay far more forceful attention to the needs of the cities than is presently the case. The cities need greater help from the Federal government and—as the emerging centers of an urban nation—they are entitled to it.

They need more than fresh revenues, although that need is the most critical. They need greater co-operation in reaching regional agreements to remedy regional problems. They need committee-level representation in both Houses of Congress. But most of all, the cities need a reassessment, a redirection, of Federal attitudes and programs to grant the metropolitan areas their due share of the nation's domestic expenditures.

The dislocations inherent in adjusting the national perspective to the cities will be painful and not readily accomplished. But I believe these changes are imperative. For the United States of the nineteen-sixties should not be remembered by future generations as a country that won supremacy in outer space but lost the struggle for a better way of life in its cities.

Index

Senators, Republican, 130-131
Sheffield, Frederic, 11, 134
Siam, 98
Sibal, Abner, 126
"Silk Stocking" district (*see* New
York City, 17th District)
Skybolt program, 77
Slavery, 72, 98
Smith Act, 47
Sobeloff, Simon E., 7
Socialism, 84
Soviet Union, 123
Spoils system, 119
State legislatures, 68
States, and civil rights, 36
and Supreme Court, 68, 71
Statesmen, 104, 113, 122
Statutes, criminal, 34
state, 36
Stimson, Henry, 121-122
Stimson Doctrine, 121
Suburbs, 143-144
Swing, General Joseph, 7, 49, 101

Taft, Robert A., 120
Taft, Robert A., Jr., 120-121
Taft, William Howard, 39, 119-120
Taiwan, aid to, 83
Taney, Chief Justice, 72
Taxes and taxation, 72, 144
Thayer, Walter, 134
Theater, 10-11, 28-29
Tibet and Tibetans, 101-102
Trade, world, 85-86
Travel, freedom to, 41, 54-65, 115
Triborough Bridge and Tunnel Authority, 108
Truman, Harry S., 99, 122-123

Underdeveloped nations, 83-86, 88-90
United Nations, 65, 89, 103
General Assembly, 123
Security Council, 123
United Nations Charter, 123
United States, common law in, 36
and Europe, 75-82
and foreign affairs, 123

foreign aid given by, 82-95
foreign policy of, 91-92, 122-123
foreign relations of, 56
immigration to, 96-103
in nineteenth century, 91
and United Nations, 65
United States banks, 72
United States Commissioner of Immigration and Naturalization, 49
United States Congress, 19-31, 118
and cities, 144-145
and civil rights, 36, 40
committee chairmen in, 24-25
communication in, 24
compared with House of Commons, 23-24
and confidential information, 48-49
85th, 60
87th, 26
and the electorate, 20-21
and Executive branch, 58
and foreign aid, 82
and foreign nations, 76
and immigration, 97-101, 103
and individual liberties, 51
Minority in, 22, 41-42
power structure of, 25-26, 41
question and answer periods in, 24
Republican leadership in, 22
role of, 58
Rules Committee, 26
running for, 1-2, 8-18, 28-29
and Supreme Court, 66, 68-72
weaknesses of, 21-23
(*See also* U.S. House of Representatives; U.S. Senate)
United States Constitution, 34-36, 62-63
enforcement of, 34, 39
Fifth Amendment to, 50, 56, 59, 64
First Amendment to, 34-35, 50, 55, 59, 61-62, 64
interpretation of, 71
Ninth Amendment to, 62